Who Would I Be
If I Weren't So Afraid?

Ginger Grancagnolo, Ed.D., D. Min.

BALBOA.
PRESS

A DIVISION OF HAY HOUSE

Balboa Press books may be ordered through booksellers or by contacting:

Balboa Press
A Division of Hay House
1663 Liberty Drive
Bloomington, IN 47403
www.balboapress.com
1-(877) 407-4847

ISBN: 978-1-4525-3910-2 (sc)
ISBN: 978-1-4525-3909-6 (hc)
ISBN: 978-1-4525-3911-9 (ebk)
Library of Congress Control Number: 2011915867

The ideas represented herein are the personal interpretation of the author and are not necessarily endorsed by the copyright holder of *A Course in Miracles*®. Portions from *A Course in Miracles*, © copyright 1975, reprinted by permission of the Foundation for Inner Peace, Inc., PO Box 598, Mill Valley, CA 94942.

Biblical quotations are from *The Jerusalem Bible* (Garden City, NY: Doubleday, 1966).

Printed in the United States of America

Balboa Press rev. date: 09/15/2011

CONTENTS

To my mother, affectionately known as "Mama Novena"; she is my best friend and a vibrant example of determination, wisdom, faith, and good, old-fashioned neighborhood loving.

Acknowledgments

To Carol, Angel, and Elaine: They are my high-school buddies. We grew up through each other. Through tears and laughter, we are forever friends. To Vickie, my Barringer High School "boss." She unconditionally loves me and believed in me long before I did. To my cousin Cina, who is more than a sister. We hold each other's deepest secrets and dreams. She helped me shape my vision. To Fran, my assistant, who is always there with endless hours of loving deeds. To Sue, my dearest friend—she guides my course through her silent strength. Her heart is filled with God's love and her ways helped me not to be afraid. And, finally, to Fr. Albert Gorayeb, my forever priest, teacher, friend. He released my power and my faith and taught me to feel how much God loves me. May his memory remain forever.

Introduction

Fear is normal, right? That's what I used to think. How would it be to have a life without fear? Who would *you* be if you weren't so afraid? What part does fear play in our lives? What is it that we are so afraid of?

These are not the questions I asked myself early on in life, certainly not in the middle of my panic attacks or anxieties, or definitely not while I was sitting in high school with sweaty palms, praying that I wouldn't fail another test, that I wouldn't be caught with another anxiety attack just as I was going to be called on. I didn't even know enough to ask these questions. All I knew was that deep inside of me there was a tremor I couldn't get rid of. All I knew was that I had something to hide; maybe it was a defect, maybe it was low intelligence, insecurity, no self-esteem, no confidence. But none of the labels gave an indication for a cure or relief for any of the tension that racked my body by the time I was fifteen.

So it's normal, isn't it? How could we be so certain that we must have fear in our lives when people don't even know how to function without it?

In the pages that follow, I want to present a pathway to personal victory that is available for everyone. In my early days I probably called myself shy or insecure or not as intelligent or as bright as most other people. Now I understand that there was a fear in me, that there is a true definition of that fear, and there's also a remedy for it. Now I can understand that the power that I have within me cannot be taken or shaken by any external circumstance or situation. No person, place, or thing is stronger than my own power. This, of course, I now can say with great confidence after a journey of over twenty-five years in learning, researching, meditating, and praying every day.

And what I'd like to do for you is possibly to present a new definition of fear, a new window that people can look through, regardless of the degree of their fear, and not only find a better definition but a practical situation illustrated by my own experience and a workable solution for you. I'd like to help remove the pain and suffering that comes from failure that fear seems to breed and perpetuate—even in our sleep—even as we think of whatever it is that we're afraid of in some subconscious form, while we appear to function quite effectively in the outer world every day.

The path I will show you will have a faith atmosphere. My own is Judeo-Christian. What I have found is that the Author of Life is universal—a loving light, a personal, caring, loving power that breathes when we breathe and walks when we walk. What I have found is that if we can tap into the true essence of this spiritual wellspring that is within us, given to us at birth, we can come to experience it and see how the power works through us.

Once you learn how that power works through us, I'll offer very practical techniques and new thinking strategies, using our human potentials, to handle fear from the simplest things, such as: fear of going on an interview, fear of waiting for the results of a test, fear of failing, fear of public speaking, fear of intimacy, fear of dying, etc.

In these pages, I hope you will have a personal experience with that Inner Light and feel its sensitivity, its loving ability, and come to know your true self. I want you to know that you are not a failure and that fear is not only conquerable but dissolvable.

I know that as you begin to read this, you might say, "I've heard this before" or "This sounds like it's too good to be true." If it weren't for my own personal experiences in this battle with fear, I'd probably think the same way. In a way, I was my first student. I learned by working out my own problems and struggling through my own fears and failures. In fact, I was too afraid, too anxiety-ridden to even ask for help. Perhaps you've felt this way too. I felt that this had to be part of some divine plan, part of my own destiny, that I should just find it within myself and grow out of it, and that this would somehow bring about some relief and release for others who commonly suffer from fear, tension, and other anxieties.

I invite you to step through the doors of your own personal darkness and see the dawn I have seen. Learn with me to conquer the weaknesses and the failures that you think you simply have to live with. *We do not see things as they are; we see them as we are.* Through these pages, your perception of yourself will change. You will come to a deeper understanding of yourself in terms of how you were created, in terms of your true talents and abilities, and even in terms of a purpose for your life that you never thought you'd ever be able to identify or even attain.

Antoine de Saint-Exupéry said in *The Little Prince*: "It is only with the heart that one can see rightly. What is essential is invisible to the eye. The best part of you, you have not yet visited—the place of beauty and power where truly no fear exists."

Part I

Living in Fear

Chapter One

The Endless Dance with Demons

What Happened To Me

The worst of it, as far as I can recall, was in 1975 when in my own way I thought I had lost a sense of perspective or reality. I thought I had lost a sense of who I really was. In fact, I was so riveted in fear I could no longer focus on any one point or thought or feeling for more than a minute at a time. I lived in fear that racked my body, that gave me chest pains, stomach distress, difficulty in swallowing, and headaches that finally ended in a migraine that lasted for almost three weeks. I was ashen to look at, weak, without rest, unable to eat, and I got to a point where I thought the only alternative was simply to not live. I lost the focus of where anything was right or wrong, where there was power, where there was a sense of self that could bring me back to reality. I felt totally disconnected from everything and everyone around me.

Perhaps the sharpest irony is that I continued to function—quite normally, according to everyone else—as a high-school English teacher in an inner-city school in Newark called Barringer High School. I remember in between classes having to go into the ladies' room, wash my hands and face, and look in the mirror and say, "You're going to make it. Just two more classes. Just one more class, then you can go home and hide." I'd rinse my face with cold water just so that I could have the sense of touch, so I could know that my body was real and I was not just a thought. I'd take a deep breath, not knowing if I could exhale. I'd walk out into the hall, face thirty to thirty-five kids, and begin to try to explain the parts of speech.

What brought that chapter in my life to a close was when I visited a teacher that I had had in high school. She was my art teacher and my religion teacher. Her name is Sr. Joanne Ryan. I went to Mount Saint Dominic Academy, a very achievement-oriented private Catholic school for girls. I loved the school. I loved the safety in the walls and in the uniforms that we all wore. The friends I made in high school are still my closest and dearest friends. We hide each other's secrets and we know each other's faults and strengths; yet even with all of that bonding, those were the most frightening days of my life.

You see, I had a learning disability. If I were in grammar school now, perhaps I would be labeled as dyslexic. I had problems reading. The letters would jump and twist. My eyes would fix and immediately I could hear myself say, "I'll fail." At that moment, it was like somebody pulled the switch or pulled the plug on the computer, and my brain literally shut down. My heart would continue to pound, the sweat would pour from my palms, and almost every paper I passed in to the teacher was curled up on the edges like a Dead Sea Scroll. I was frightened most of the day in high school, but I hid it. I covered it with a sense of humor. I was the class clown. It was easier for me to be the class clown and to fail because I broke up the class—I made everyone laugh and then the teacher would send me out of the room—than to be caught with a D or an F on my paper and have a note sent home and the grades posted on the bulletin board for all to view. That was a death that I was not willing to die—and so, I died a little every day. I began to dance with the demon from way back then. I had had elements of this happening in grammar school, but I had not detected it. But by the time the pressure was on in high school, I could feel the demon breathing down my neck, saying, "Soon I will ask you to dance and it will never end."

And so this teacher, Sister Joanne, was one of the few people I can recall in all those high-school years who had a way of looking at me, of looking through me and saying, "Someday you're going to realize who you are and all this will fade." She had confidence in me. She took a little extra time to say, "Just do your best and it will be okay. Your fear will dissolve when you learn to relax a little more." I didn't know what she was saying at the time, but I certainly appreciated the little extra attention that she gave me and the fact that she respected me and kept my secret well.

I graduated, even went on to college, but the fear remained. Then at one point, when I was twenty-five years old, I had a migraine headache that lasted for three weeks. The pain was unbearable. A friend—from high school, I might add—came to visit. She didn't know what to do with me. I was sitting and rocking with my fist in my mouth, trying not to scream from the pain. She thought if she took me out to get some fresh air and sunlight that it might help me. Well, we hadn't been outdoors more than ten or fifteen minutes when I said to her, "Elaine, please, I want you to take me somewhere."

Well, the thought of this nun came to me. My friend drove me back to the high school. I didn't know if Sister Joanne was even still there; years had passed and we had lost contact. But anyway, I rang the bell, and as I opened the door the familiar smell of the cleanliness of the school, the shininess of the marble floors, the ornateness of the furniture started to calm me again, because I had been made to feel safe in those days by the surroundings of the school. It was the unsafe feeling I had in myself that caused the pain. I asked the receptionist, "Can I see Sr. Joanne Ryan, please?" She looked at me and she said, "Yes, just a moment."

A little time passed and she escorted me into an office that had again an ornate appeal to it, with tapestries hanging on the wall, several familiar faces of some saints or bishops whom I could never identify, and there Sister Joanne sat on the other side of the desk with the same soft face and gentle eyes. We spoke briefly. I don't know what enabled me to just blurt out my pain, but I did. I told her of the pain in my head. We talked briefly and she taught me an exercise that day. The whole meeting took no longer than thirty minutes. She sat me in a chair and she said to me, "Please just listen and be silent." She began to ask me to close my eyes and simply take a deep breath and breathe in and breathe out, and she went through a type of breathing and relaxing exercise. I followed it. I followed in the trust that she had always indicated to me and always given to me through the years of high school.

It was a very simple exercise, one that used a blue-white light as a source of imagery and peace, some soft, gentle words, and in a matter of moments the exercise was over. I opened my eyes and, even though it was brief, I began to feel better. I thanked her. She wrote out the exercise for me and asked me to take a program. She said, "Go and take this class. It's called the Silva Method.[1] I'd like you to go and take it with the teacher that I took it with. His name is Fr. Albert Gorayeb, and he's teaching this program in St. Ann's Church in West Paterson, New Jersey." And so I took the paper and left.

Within a few hours after that, my migraine headache completely disappeared. It disappeared in a way that I didn't even notice. My thoughts shifted. Before I noticed, the pain was gone. I started to think more about this class. I started to think more about the fact that there was help for me at a time when I thought I was so desperate. I continued to practice the exercise she gave me. I practiced it lying flat on the floor. Anxious moments did come again. This wasn't a panacea, such that in a few short moments a magic wand was waved over me and it was gone, puff, forever. The anxiety continued, but not with the same intensity.

---

[1] Jose Silva, *The Silva Mind Control Method* (New York: Simon & Schuster, 1977).

In November of 1975, I followed the Silva Method program for the first time. In this program, I learned how to use my brain and my mind in a way that has permanently changed my life. It taught me that science and divine intelligence can meet hand-in-hand and serve life toward success, peace, and health.

How You See It

Those were the days that I look back at now, and in fact I keep those memories close to me because they help me get in touch with where humanity hurts the most. They help me to stay very sensitive and compassionate to the single thread that runs through all of us, the fact that day by day it's common for us to dance—in our minds—with the demon called fear, an inner phantom that we cannot identify or describe, yet has total control over us.

You can awaken in the middle of the night and find that demon there at the foot of your bed, haunting you, making your heart pound, making you think you hear sounds—that you see sights, flashes, images. You can waken in the early morning expecting a great day and yet have, again, a haunting refrain of some past memory when you failed, when you fell flat on your face and didn't know why, other than that you kept calling it some fear inside—something inside that runs you, that in fact owns you.

For those of us who have these thoughts, they hold us back from progress and our lives. They hold us back from enjoying the simplest things: sharing a meal with friends, experiencing real tears and real laughter. We are relentlessly robbed of the effervescence that we really want in our lives. We watch our lives like we're watching a movie—touching nothing, being affected by nothing. Meanwhile, this phantom continues to burrow itself somewhere in our bodies, causing stress and stomach disorders, sweats, physical anxieties, nervous twitches, blood pressure changes, panic attacks, and, in some cases, the loss of a true sense of the reality of who we are and what we're capable of.

The interesting thing about all of this is that fear, in its luminous definition, seems to have a power over us that we do not have over ourselves. We see it as something that is inside and yet outside at the same time. It stops us from being confident on a job interview, from being able to smile at strangers, from hugging our children too much, from being kind to the person who just opened the door for us. It stops us from asking for that job promotion, when in our hearts we know we're probably the best qualified.

Along with this everyday occurrence, fear has its roots somewhere inside the human mind and its effect in the body. As we watch the news, we are reinforced to believe in fear, that it is an enemy and has legions and legions of soldiers that we will never be able to defeat. As we read the newspapers, our fears again are compounded. We become physically afraid, emotionally afraid, financially, mentally, and spiritually afraid. In all layers of life, all we do is dance with this demon, hoping somewhere it will end but not knowing how to end it, where even to begin.

We try to use our coping skills, but sometimes—most of the time—to no avail. We try to take days off from work, read a book, get involved in self-help, perhaps try counseling, prayer, or meditation. But somehow the root, the cause, seems to grow back faster than crabgrass. It seems as if fear is an acceptable behavior pattern, a normal habit. In fact, if you think about it, do you know a person who is peaceful and lives mostly in this peaceful condition? Do you know a person who has an inner confidence—not an arrogance, but a confidence—that seems gentle and unshakable? Do you know an individual whose peace you can feel even in the face of adversity and struggle?

Where do we go to learn how to conquer this fear? What I have learned in my own dance with the demon fear is that fear is not to be conquered; rather, fear is to be reviewed as a signal that your power as a human being is being drained away by a person, a place, or a thing. Fear has to be redefined in a way that makes it conquerable, desirable, dissolvable. In fact, as we continue in later chapters, it will be my intention to help you to recognize fear as a signal of change that you will befriend, not be frightened by. Life consists of change, and most of fear is wrapped around that concept of change and the unknown. In later chapters, we will define many faces of fear, the kinds of fear that we have, and show specifically what it does to us. But for now, let us just focus on the pain of the fear, really get in touch in our bodies where we have felt trapped, confused, stuck, threatened.

What It Really Is

The first place of change, in order to dissolve fear, must be in the body. That's where you first feel the fear, and then it gets manifested in behavior. Sometimes the fearful thought or feeling can happen so simultaneously, I literally don't know which one is happening first. I'm so swept away by this demon's move that I didn't even know I was tangled in its dance. But I feel it in my chest; my throat is closing; I'm getting the pains in my stomach; I'm getting the tension headache or the migraine headache.

I'd like to present a workable definition—not an absolute definition—of fear, one which will help us to reframe the fear and failure syndrome. As I've experienced it in my own life, here's what I believe fear is:

> **Fear is the picture I make in my mind that makes it look like I'll fail, I'll lose, or I'm not safe.**

Look at the first part of that definition: "Fear is the picture." Here's where the demon has its way. If I'm in a situation, looking through the filter of fear, I've lost true self-perception. As my imagination adheres me to that image or reflection, to those faces that seem to threaten me, the places that I think will somehow make me feel unsafe, I cannot determine the difference between the illusion that fear has now given me and the true picture.

Furthermore, my body biologically doesn't know the difference between imagination and fact.[2] In fact, it has been proven that when given imagination or fact, the brain perceives imagination first. The brain functions through imagery. An example might be if we simply say the words *apple, beach, chair.* What comes to mind is not the spelling of those words, *a-p-p-l-e, b-e-a-c-h, c-h-a-i-r,* but rather images of those objects. You are then connected to those images. Your body responds to those images by the value you have placed upon them, either positive or negative. In the moment of fear, the demon wraps its arms around me through that photo in my imagination. If what I see in my mind creates a picture, even though it's an illusion that makes it look like I'm going to fail, I'm going to lose, or I'm not safe, I will then literally release a biochemical reaction in my body that further reinforces the fact that even though it's a picture in my mind, I will now begin to believe it.

A perfect example of this is through dreams. We've all had the common experience of waking up from a dream in which we are running. What we notice is that when we awaken from the dream, the heart is beating at a rapid pace. Logic tells us that our hearts don't beat at a rapid pace during sleep, but it's through the photography in the imagination that the heart has actually increased in its rate of speed. This happens in a matter of moments, and so when I see this picture in my mind, my body creates evidence that says, "Look out, you are in a fight-flight response; you are in a fight-flight challenge situation." At this moment, what is now lost is the truth—the truth about the situation and the truth about myself. The ability to meet any challenge is lost. The chemistry in my body is flowing, the adrenaline flowing, and the demon grips harder now. I am caught in the catch-22. The more my body responds, the more my imagination

---

[2]   Silva, *The Silva Mind Control Method,* 65-66.

sees real threat, and, in fact, I am lost in the picture in my mind. What actually may be happening may be, at that moment, out of my grasp of understanding.

Let's take the typical job interview. Here you are, ready to go on the interview. You've selected the right outfit. Even as you're selecting the right outfit or what you think might be the appropriate attire, what runs through your mind is the picture that it probably won't be suitable; it probably will not be approved of by the interviewer or the corporation. As you're literally putting on the clothes, you are putting on, in your mind, the picture of the failure. Now, you try to talk over that picture. "Everything will go fine; everything will be fine. I've got my resume; I've got my letters of reference. I'm going to say the best thing." You rehearse it over and over, but your first impression is the one that wins, the one that says, "They probably won't like me; I'm probably going to lose; I'm probably not going to be their first pick." That's the one that went into the very cells of the body and now actually is owned by you. Again, the biochemical response is working and so the adrenaline is pumping, the heart is pounding, the dry mouth continues. Hard to swallow as it is, you try to speak and practice your rehearsed lines over and over so that you will sound like the best selection for this job. You may or may not get the job; you may or may not even have wanted the job. This is really not the issue. The issue is the dynamics of how your imagination, brain, and mind have so worked together to work you up into letting that demon have this dance with you, through that interview, into the night, into the day, waiting the response of your acceptance or your rejection.

Even if you talk to friends to help remove these images, while sometimes it's helpful it's only fleeting, because while they're talking to you they may help you to feel better, but once you hear the click of the receiver on the phone the image in your mind is back. The demon dances on and on. You almost can hear a chuckle. If you try hard enough, you can almost envision the phantom leaning heavily on your chest, making it hard for you to breathe once again.

Another interesting point about fear is that whether it is for a happy event, a good event, or a negative, unpleasant event, we can still have the same reactions. Maybe this is a first-date situation or the reacquainting with someone you haven't seen in a long time. If you have a picture in your mind that says, "You'll fail, you'll lose, you're not safe," you will again dance on and on with the phantom that lives in your imagination. A happy event might be something as simple as a high school reunion where people can gather again and laugh about old times and about the loss of hairlines and added lines around their faces, and everyone probably goes through a process of looking in the mirror and worrying what they will say. "Is someone going to be heavier than I am? Be more successful?" Again, these images cloak you and the dagger of the demon begins to stab you in the chest, stab in your gut, preventing you from having, perhaps, the time of your life just collecting again with friends who were once so important to you, and maybe even some of them are still with you now.

Another example of this endless dance can happen to us, certainly, with finances. Look at what happens to us when we get close to the date when bills or taxes are due. Look at how many times we repeat the story of whether we can or can't afford something, and the truth about it is, for the most part, when the day comes somehow the money is available, and even if it isn't you know at that point you'll have to think in a logical manner to be able to handle it. Even at that crucial point, fear will not create a lump of money on your desk, enabling you to pay the bill. We know this logically, of course, but the demon intoxicates us. The phantom lives in the night and talks to you, whispers into your ear to tell you what a failure you are for not being financially solvent, for not having managed your affairs in a better way.

What kind of parent are you? What kind of spouse, businessperson, etc.? On and on it goes, and always the demon focuses on the same fact: "If I think I'll fail, I'll lose, or I'm not safe, the demon can dance with me. By day and by night, I am stuck, endlessly trapped in the arms of this phantom, freezing me to failure, robbing me of my true sense of who I am and who I can be."

Look at how the demon works through media and the news. Every night we sit at home watching the nightly news, watching one violent story after another, one more racial outbreak, one more rape, one more child being abused, one more drug-infested crack house that has ruined the future of a community. Now, what we do is mentally assess that life will never change. What we do, because of that image, is sleep on it and wake up in the morning expecting another hopeless day of violence and crime and racism. When I take these images into my mind, without realizing it I create an atmosphere in my body that sets up a further hopelessness in the way I will carry out my day. In short, I rob myself of the power to change any situation into a more peaceful and productive end result. So, even if I think I'm detached by sitting in front of the television, I'm not. Those images stay with me.

Let's face it: We're the first generation who have watched several wars on television. Whether they were racial or international or in the Middle East, we've watched them. We have now become a society which believes that just as much as fear is a part of life, war and racism will never die. Yet, if we were to fill out a survey, "Do you want peace in the world?" I can't think of a single person who'd say, "No, I don't." How could we want peace and not believe that we can make it happen? How could we want peace and want to end this, and then in the same breath rob peace in our own bodies, keep ourselves on our last nerve as we go out into the world? We're adding to the threat rather than adding to the solution.

The demon of fear knows no boundary and even kisses God in the face. Many of us, as it now has been proven through surveys, believe in the existence of God,[3] believe that God is a power greater than ourselves and is a power that creates and promotes life, that in fact

---

[3] Joan Borysenko, *Fire in the Soul* (New York: Warner, 1993), 26-28.

this power created the universe and has a sense of divine intelligence, has a sense that creates an intelligence even in our own bodies. Look at the function of your body, for example. It's not common for an average person to know, for example, the functions of the liver, how many lobes of the brain there are, or the connection between kidney and gall bladder. This is truly a masterpiece of how all these cells interconnect. Even from watching the conception of life, where the egg meets the sperm and forms a cell, through a microscopic lens, we do not understand how that tiny, tiny spot of life develops into the full person. There is order and intelligence there.

We see this in the seasons, the cycles of growth, as trees and leaves die only to be born again. We have a sense of nature, that we are connected to nature and connected to the universe, and somehow through this there is a presence that we call God, the Author of Life. For some of us, our connection to this spiritual sense still resonates with a fire and brimstone attitude, so that we are afraid of the very presence that we need to go to in search of answers. We oftentimes will be afraid of punishment, like God randomly selecting who shall be the favorite that day or will have his or her prayers answered. If we look, perhaps there is some personal evidence to this idea, if we think of how many have prayed and whatever it is that they have prayed for simply seemed to have not been answered—or it felt like no one was even listening. Even our connection with this spiritual source is vague and confusing, yet we want to, at some level, connect with this God. Naturally, there is confusion in wanting to draw close to power and yet be frightened by it, all in the same breath.

Throughout history, our approach towards coming to know this power is through learning about God through books, famous works, etc. It's my personal experience that the best way to learn about this power is to let the power teach you from within; from your heart, from a deep place inside where you couldn't have created rules and regulations and definitions about God that simply are not true because they're rooted in limitation and conditions, while the true power of life, in its essence, remains truth, goodness, and promoting of good for all concerned.

Some of the experiences I've had have helped me to overcome fear and its failures. Let's go back to the definition:

Fear is the picture I make in my mind that makes it look like I'll lose, I'll fail, or I'm not safe.

Knowing that there is an intelligence in all of life, I must start with an antidote to that definition of fear. The antidote is in an affirmation. An affirmation is a positive sentence I tell myself. It has been shown through educational psychology and the study of behavior that whatever we continue to say frequently we become, much like a self-fulfilling prophecy.[4]

What we need to practice as a first antidote to fear is the language that we use when speaking about ourselves to ourselves. As a practice, the first antidote is the affirmation:

I see the truth in everything I do, say, think, and feel.

It is recommended here that, regardless of your fear or anxiety, you write this affirmation ten times daily. A minimum amount of time for this to soak in and really begin to change your attitude is about a month. In some cases, you may need to write it more. There is truth within you. There is a power. Simply begin by speaking to yourself about yourself in a new way. Use a common notebook. Write the affirmation three times in the morning, three in the afternoon, three or four times at night. Sometimes what is also helpful is to make index cards—nice and big, like 5 x 8—and write out this affirmation, placing it on the refrigerator, in your bathroom, on the

---

[4]   Robert A. Harper, *Psychoanalysis and Psychotherapy* (Englewood Cliffs, NJ: Prentice-Hall, 1959), 67-68.

visor of the car, on the bulletin board at work, on the nightstand, on your mirror in your room, anywhere it's visible. Let your mind take a picture of it and reaffirm you're going to see the truth. Through this simple sentence, you are putting belief back in yourself that you are as you are created, an intelligent person with a good heart. This begins to weaken the strength in the demon and to slow down the dance that has caused you near inertia in the past.

Your Worksheet

Now it's your turn. This is a brief relaxation exercise that I suggest you use on a regular, daily basis, regardless of the intensity of the peace or anxiety on any given day. It serves, again, as an antidote to the fact that we do live in a stressful life.

- Begin by sitting upright in a comfortable position. Let your back be supported by the chair, then close your eyes. Just keep your eyes closed. Begin to breathe as you normally do, breathing in and breathing out. Your only focus in these initial moments is to simply notice the breathing. Notice only the breathing. If it helps, place your hand on your chest and watch the movement of your chest, rising and then declining as you breathe in and breathe out. Then continue by saying,

I see the truth in everything I do, say, think, and feel.

- Repeat it again. Repeat the affirmation three times slowly.
- Count from one to three and create a picture of some place where you feel very peaceful and calm and relaxed. At this point, sometimes people picture a favorite vacation spot, a park, a beach, a wooded area, an open meadow, sitting by the side of a stream and hearing the sounds of the gurgling

brook. Hear nature around you, the sounds of birds. Feel the golden sunshine kissing around your forehead and relaxing you.

- Repeat to yourself, three times:

  There is peace within me and this peace is a goodness, a power, that will never change.

- Repeat it three times, then repeat three times again:

  I see the truth in everything I do, say, think, and feel.

- Finally, as a concluding sentence, you will simply say to yourself:

  The peace and the calm confidence that I feel now shall remain with me throughout this day and this night.

- Then, when you are comfortable to do so, simply open your eyes. As you are opening your eyes, you will say:

  I am safe, no matter what.

You see, these images of peace and calm and confidence shrink the demon, cripple his dancing legs, weaken his arms. He no longer has a grasp on you. It is recommended that you do this exercise every day on a regular basis. It's even recommended that you take this exercise and in your own words record it into a tape recorder. Then you can take the cassette with you to work and perhaps at lunchtime, sitting in a quiet place or pulling the car over to the side of the road, simply take a few moments and listen. It is recommended that you listen to this tape, or repeat this exercise in your own way, after work, at the end of the day.

This exercise doesn't have negative side effects. The more you use this basic exercise, the more you will dissolve the fear, shrink and cripple the demon. You will stand alone, inside yourself, feeling calm and confident, watching the phantom fade.

Chapter Two

The Demon with a Thousand Faces

What Happened To Me

Nothing real can be threatened. Nothing unreal exists.
Herein lies the peace of God.[5]

When I first read this back in 1981, it was my first reality check. I had to read it several times, over and over, until I could finally actually feel in my mind this magnificent cord moving from the seat of my soul, deep inside my heart, directly to the Creator and feel the safety that was promised because this is the truth, and feel that life-giving source pouring through me every time I breathe, knowing that if I would see that picture first and then make my own personal decisions, that my decisions would be based on a more congruent than incongruent model.

When I got to the last line, then I moved to the second: "Nothing unreal exists." In that single instant, that moment of heightened awareness, I saw my worries begin to dissolve, and what remained was just the truth about me, that I am good and I have value because

---

[5]   Foundation for Inner Peace, Introduction to *A Course in Miracles* (Farmingdale, NY: Coleman, 1975).

19

I was created and the power within me is part of the universe. Finally, when I got to the third line, "Herein lies the peace of God," a deepened sense of this awareness rushed through my whole body, and I could feel the light in every cell. "Herein lies the peace of God": in my mind I saw *p-i-e-c-e*. In that moment I felt one with God.

I've read these lines in happy days, in calm days, and certainly have looked for them to go back and read them in the days when I felt most vulnerable. And always when I come to the end line, "Herein lies the peace of God," I can feel the truth beginning again to flourish within me. I then change my mind about the way that I am seeing a given situation. I then change my perspective on a solution that I might have had only ten minutes earlier. I then can change my perception and let a truth come through me that says, "Unless you carry peace, you will not dictate peace through your life. Unless you breathe in peace, all your reactions to life will be somehow a further perpetuation of violence and attack-and-be-attacked relationships." Unless we make a commitment to come to know the truth about ourselves and stay in that focus, we will be frightened, out-of-focus beings moving from one vulnerable situation to the next, aging with every hour.

Once I was determined to stay on this path, I uncovered the layers that fear used to keep me wrapped up in failure. After defining fear, I was able to dissolve this demon with a thousand faces into one. For me, the most powerful antidote to powerlessness came from accepting *A Course In Miracles*, which helped me understand that "Nothing real can be threatened. Nothing unreal exists. Herein lies the peace of God." And perception makes for projection.

How You See It

Where does fear come from anyway? Is it really a natural part of us, a normal part, something that we have to live with? Is this the original sin of the twenty-first century, that we have to be frightened and feel so threatened by all of the external forces, the environment, economy, fear of abuse, fear of disease, fear of losing someone, fear of not being successful enough, pretty enough, tall enough? Where does all this come from?

The question here, perhaps, is: Are we born in fear or out of fear? Do we learn to become frightened, threatened, so vulnerable as we grow older? Is it part of the natural aging process?

Perhaps these questions can become more simplified and possibly even clarified with our definition:

Fear is the picture I make in my mind that makes it look like I'll fail, I'll lose, or I'm not safe.

The key phrase here is "picture in my mind." Is it possible that the picture in one's mind can be transferred from generation to generation, much like blue eyes or physical stature or a propensity for music or art? If this were the case, then we would have a better understanding of how certain people seem to be born with more confidence, while others seem to be shy, more introverted. Many early schoolteachers tell us that they can track as early as kindergarten and first grade how a child who is seemingly shy, shut off from the rest, off into the corner, can spend years in this vulnerable position before finally maturing and reaching some level of confidence, perhaps as late as even into college and some maybe never at all, while others seem to be born leaders, out into the front, little ones who are in charge of their own world, almost like a natural instinct.

More and more research shows us that there is a physiological genetic coding as well as a biological genetic coding, which means that the child in utero develops the physical characteristics from the chromosomal components of both mother and father, as well as their attitudinal dispositions.[6] Sometimes this is not seen so clearly

---

6   Lawrence B. Schiamberg, *Human Development* (New York: Macmillan, 1985), 55-71.

in infancy, but shortly thereafter, as the child begins to exert power and demonstrate ability. Even before language, before the age of two or three, the personality seems to take shape, and many parents have said that even in early infancy their children seem to imitate one or both of the parents. Some psychologists have said that this comes from modeling, which is an imitative pattern, while others now are saying that this, in fact, is coming from the coding of the DNA while the fetus is still in utero. If this is the case, it would seem, then, that we are born with a predisposition and, on top of that, are also subjected to learning behavior patterns.

I would say that the truth lies somewhere in between, much like the age-old expression that "history repeats itself" is true simply because human nature has not drastically changed over the years, but rather seems to repeat its same weaknesses, its same vulnerabilities, its same view of the world in components of good and evil. This would apply as we see the evidence of generations and generations of alcoholics and generations and generations of abuse victims then giving birth to more victimizers, and so this fear line moving from generation to generation is also quite a possibility.

Again, if we go back to the definition we would see that fear comes from a perception. If fear comes from a perception of how I view myself, and how I view myself in my early days comes from how I have been taught to see myself, again there is evidence that there is a combination of being born in a sense as well as learning fearful reactions. How could it really be the truth that fear is interwoven into the chromosomal makeup, when for centuries and centuries we have always philosophized about human potential, its power, the power to think, the power of great achievers who appear every century, such as Albert Schweitzer, Ghandi, Mother Teresa, Martin Luther King? These are examples of people who have overcome vulnerabilities.

Does it really matter, then, when we see that in every decade, every century, there are people who have overcome the worst of circumstances, confronted fear whether it was born or learned through their experience? How could it be, then, that these people have not weakened to the fear factor? What is it in them that forced them to move forward, to confront, and to conquer? I believe it is the picture that they make in their minds. Remember our definition:

Fear is the picture I make in my mind that makes it look like I'll fail, I'll lose, or I'm not safe.

With this definition, clearly, we can see that perception of one's self will dictate reactions and decisions, as well as values. This can also dispel some prior understandings about faces, about fear, that make it seem that fear has separate categories, such as the fear of heights, a fear of closed-in places, a fear of water, a fear of commitment. This sounds like there are endless lists of fears that people have and, at best, what you could do is try to get one that doesn't limit you too much, so that it will simply be as ordinary as the common cold or the occasional headache, something that you just have to deal with, never really knowing what is the root or origin of the fear.

From my own personal experiences, what I have come to understand is that there is but one face of fear, and it is the perception that you are powerless in a given situation over something outside of yourself. Literally, what you do—through this picture, through this visual imagery in your mind, based on the perception of yourself—is you believe wholeheartedly that a person, place, or thing is stronger or more powerful than yourself, and so it will conquer you, it will weaken you, it will make you sick, it will win, it will cause you to fail, it will let your body crumble, it will weaken your ability to think and use that natural human potential to see through from problem to solution.

All fear, then, has but one face. It is a distortion of your personal power. Note here that when I say personal power, I mean that it is your power as a person, a power as you have been created to be a full person, and so this personal power is a combination of human and spiritual powers, spiritual powers meaning that the breath of life within you is from the power of the Author of Life, and that you are always connected to that force. Whenever we lose sight of the invisible umbilical cord of light from ourselves, deep inside from the seat of our soul, connecting us to the Author of Universe, whenever we lose sight of that, we lose sight of our personal power, our power to be people.

From this, it is easy to see that the minute we walk out into the world, a person who looks better, has more money, prestige, fame, or fortune could threaten us. A place too high, too closed in, too wide open, could threaten us. A thing, such as a train, a plane, a fast-moving vehicle, an elevator, could threaten us, because in that moment what we are experiencing is the illusion that there is something outside in these persons, places, and things that could literally annihilate us in a single blow. In that moment, we are experiencing a separation from our true self, a separation as if someone had cut the invincible umbilical cord between us and the Author of Life. Even as I am experiencing it, I am implying that this is an impossibility. It's impossible to cut the cord between you and the Author of Life.

What creates this fear? If we were clear that we're always connected with the Author of Life, what throws us off? What throws the focus into mayhem and produces several kinds of fears? The many faces of fear are simply the reflection of this one fear: There is something outside of yourself that makes you feel separated from the power source.

The common explanation of fear is given many names: agoraphobia, claustrophobia, and so forth. This seems like the dog chasing its tail, for we could go from one thing to the next and still never find an origin. I prefer to stay to the reality that we are connected to power, and that in that truth we develop in an ongoing way our expression of personal power, thereby dissolving our fears day by day. Perhaps this is best explained.

How do we get out of focus? What can throw us off, if this is the truth? The answer is: "Fear is always a sign of strain arising whenever what you want conflicts with what you do."[7] The key word is *sign*. It is a symptom of strain. Another word for *strain* is also *stress* or *dis-ease*, not being at ease, when there is something out of balance.

It's so easy to drift away from the source with the fast pace we live, the economic pressures. All of the tried-and-true structures of life have fallen, both in church and in state. The family falling apart—one dysfunctionality to the next—all of this splashed across the media tells us that we have something to fear. We have ourselves to fear. We are afraid of each other, afraid of war, afraid of nuclear holocaust, afraid of disease, and again the constant reinforcement of this makes us believers in the illusion. And so, following the second phrase of this quote, the sign of strain or out-of-balance comes when what we want conflicts with what we do. Basically, what we want is health, prosperity and happiness, and what we do is constantly reinforce the fear. We want peace and yet we live with constant attack thoughts, or fear of being attacked. We want happiness and yet our strained faces meet each other with darting eyes, afraid to even look into another person's face and give a simple smile. We want prosperity, and yet our ability to reach a balance in ourselves financially seems almost out of reach with rising costs, taxes, and unforeseen, hidden costs that can come up in any given day. So what we want and how we act are in opposition.

What you want can simply be called a *desire*, and what you do can be called a *behavior*. Whenever the desire and the behavior do not match, we create incongruity. The desire is always an internal emotional element, and what we do is always an external one. It's how we act and react. When what we have on the inside doesn't match our expressions on the outside, the whole person now is out of balance. When we're out of focus, fear takes over. The demons

---

[7]   Foundation for Inner Peace, *A Course in Miracles*, 1:25.

are back, dancing us into the night and waiting to wake us up in the morning. The end result is we do not feel safe, walk in a safety or in a peace. Rarely do our everyday expressions sound hopeful, confident, and at ease. With this understanding, we can now see that all fear distorts personal power. The personal power quotient simply goes out of focus, and the inside desire doesn't match the outside perception.

The signs of strain are everywhere, even when little children are learning to socialize. We look at elements in our society that are supposed to be about happiness, like the little league or dancing lessons, and we see how, in our distorted minds, we have imposed pressures on young children: the pressure to compete and do the best, the pressure to have the coach notice you, the pressure of having enough money to buy uniforms, or the pressure of being picked up and driven to dancing school, and the pressure to perform in the recital.

We can look at other examples as we continue on life's path and see again these incongruities, where things that are supposed to be fun, supposed to be about goodness and happiness and sharing have become distorted. Many Americans wait all year to take a one or two week vacation. There is so much stress in getting to the airport, getting all the bags on the plane, keeping the kids in line, strapped into their seats, that by the time they get there, they're exhausted. By the time they get home, they probably need a vacation from the vacation.

We're looking for the three golden stars of health and happiness and prosperity. How apparent is the distortion of health now when our government spends nearly a trillion dollars in health care a year? It's all over the media that the rising cost of health care in this country could bankrupt the nation. The message this constantly brings out is that there is something on the outside, sickness or disease, that could come at any time, like the demon in the night, and snuff out security, both in your physical health as well as in your bankbook. Yet, if I asked people what is most important to them to have a good life, most would probably put health and peace of mind first. Here's a clear example of how what we want on the outside (good health) and what we do about it on the inside conflict. We want health care in this country, and what do we do about it?

Here's another contradiction. We had a "Just Say No" antidrug campaign to help children understand drugs are bad, and yet the biggest booming industry in the country is pharmaceuticals. Of course, medication drugs are not all bad. But there's rampant abuse and overmedicating by the average consumer. If average people opened their medicine cabinets, they would see things that are toxic to the body. If they would be more congruent with what they want, they would have to take responsibility and eat better, exercise, stop drinking and smoking, and really change their lifestyles. This, however, would take an effort, and so they would rather simply take the medication, keep using the nasal sprays, the decongestants, the aspirins, the pain-relievers, rather than seeing, perhaps, that there is a nutritional imbalance within themselves, the correction of which would actually dissolve not only these uncomfortable, reoccurring and chronic symptoms, but get to the cause. We have evidence that this is the truth. In fact, natural remedies have been around longer than medicine, but once again, what we want and what we do are in conflict. When this occurs, we go out of focus. When we go out of focus, we become sitting ducks for the demon, for the phantom of fear to come and take us and put a noose around our necks. We lose our personal power. We lose our natural, innate ability to make proper decisions that lead us to good reactions, good values, and long-term positive effects.

If we look at the many faces of fear, we have to be willing to look at the many reflections of the one cause of fear, which is the individual going out of focus about power, and then multiply each person being out of focus times five billion people in the world. When out-of-focus people make decisions, the results of these decisions will certainly be a cluster of imbalanced decisions. *Chaos* is another word for this.

Isn't our world a little chaotic? Aren't there some discrepancies? How could we have a world that loves children and yet has blaring laws that scream out to us that this is not the truth? For example, a child has to wear a helmet to ride a bicycle, but right now anybody can go into a gun shop and buy a gun—on or off the streets. Everywhere you look, you will see these grave imbalances, chaos.

Are there many faces of fear? I think not. To me, there is one face of fear, and it is the one that you see in the morning when you wake up and it is the one that puts its head on the pillow at night: your own. The face of fear is the face you have given yourself whenever you have given up your natural birthright to maintain and express true powers of goodness, health, happiness, and prosperity. This is the way that we are created. This is the truth. "Nothing real can be threatened. Nothing unreal exists. Herein lies the peace of God."

What It Really Is

Staying in this focus is certainly no easy task, since most of us have been taught the irony that unless we are afraid of something, something negative will happen. How little did we know that it would take us several decades to finally understand the true dynamics in our psychological makeup that are making this statement true. We do fear getting outside of fear because we've been taught it by our mothers and our fathers. We've been taught it by our social institutions, like school and so on. Some of us have been taught to fear even God.

I have seen also in my own life that as I began to embody more and more of those beginning statements from *A Course in Miracles*, and the more that I saw the truth in it, a veil of fear still remained, and it was the fear that if I became this, if I became the peacemaker, if I truly looked out at the world through a new lens of myself, I would be rejected. I'd be different. I would perhaps be isolated. Fear is the common face, not peace. It seems as if peace is the goal toward which we strive and do almost everything in our power to walk away from.

This helped me to understand some deeper fears of really becoming an independent person, for peace and truth truly do cultivate in such a way that you belong to life in a new way. You have an understanding of your family. You have an understanding of whatever problems you might have lived through, but you can walk away because your source is not in them but in God. When that happens, other false securities fade away. The initial reaction is this fear of rejection, of being alone. Will I be alone? Will I be peaceful, yet lonely?

No, in fact the opposite occurs. You are much better able to connect to every person, because what you see in other people is something that you have in yourself, which is that same source of God that you found. This is a process, of course, that bumps into fear and agony. One of the hardest periods was when I recognized that if I would truly let the source of my life come from inside in a deep way, I would no longer look to my mother and to my father and to early childhood as the source of who I had become. I had already categorized the positives and negatives of that, but again those incongruities somehow kept me in a safe comfort zone. I was able to draw a perimeter around myself and say, "This is what I'm able to do and this is what I'm not able to do" because of my childhood, because of my mother and father, and it got to be comfortable. I had it figured out and it was comfortable. But to really go within and dissolve all lenses that create imbalance and distorted visions of who you are means that you step outside of that comfort zone. This, perhaps, is the greatest fear of all, the feeling of nakedness, of being out in the world, out into life. Even though the rewards are great, the first step is painful.

I feel that many people want to move toward this inner peace where they'll find their true independence, but the ties against letting go are so strong that we constantly fight a polarity of the fear of being too independent and the fear of being too dependent, which keeps us trapped in this limbo state, sometimes for years. I think at times we're afraid to walk toward our path of taking the inward journey, because no matter how bad the childhood might have been, there is a fear of being disloyal to your own. We are tied to our families. Even in incest and child abuse we are tied to them, and that explains children still loving abusive mothers, wives who love abusive husbands, and so on. Subconsciously we perpetuate the misery because it's our family. It might not be much, but to the human being, it's all we've got.

This polarity of independence and dependence creates an ongoing battle. It is an example of the battle of "Is the source inside of me or is it outside of me?" This is the cause of fear, the distortion of where the power is. Is it inside or is it outside? For me, I have found most clearly that the power is within. All we've done is create more paganistic idols to worship, and they confuse us, intoxicate us, and anesthetize us about where the power really is.

Your Worksheet

To help maintain the focus, continue with the basic meditation exercise in chapter one, and also write an affirmation several times a day. Write it in a journal and keep it on index cards at work, at home, in the kitchen, where you are dressing, or wherever it is easy to see in the morning and at night. The affirmation is simple and direct, but powerful:

> **I now see the truth in everything I do, say, think, and feel.**

This affirmation is one that I have used myself over and over. Wrapped in a spiritual atmosphere, by simply taking a few deep breaths and closing my eyes as I would say it, I could always go back and return to that peaceful place inside where I could once again reclaim my birthright, reclaim the feeling that I am good, I am powerful, because the Author of Life breathes within me and the signature of that author is written on every breath I take. Whenever I can feel safety in this way, from inside out, I can remain focused and all fear dissolves. Then I can see my true self and then my perception, now based in truth, will create positive reactions, good decisions, and good values.

This shifting of the focus back into source, back into center from within, does take time. That's why it is recommended that you write the affirmation several times—ten to twenty times a day for several weeks. Writing it on the index cards simply makes it easier, because all you have to do is look at the index card and say it. I've kept it in the car, on the visor. I've kept it in my purse, on the bathroom mirror, in the kitchen, on my desk at work. I had to keep the picture of truth in front of me to dissolve the demons. Slowly, one by one, they died, and what remained was just who I am as I have been created.

In time, I was able to see the true face of who I am and know its true worth, that no matter what, in any situation, I am safe because the power within me will keep me safe. Constantly relying on this helped me to make more effective decisions and choices in my life in all areas, personally as well as professionally.

One of the greatest gifts you could give yourself is to dissolve the face of fear that you have worn for so long, to know that it is just an illusion, a mask, and come to know who you are from within, so that the simple goals of health, happiness and prosperity not only are reachable, but actually become your reality.

Chapter Three

Fear and its Failures

What Happened To Me

I can remember the old fear days, when I could be sitting comfortably at any given time and a thought would flash across my mind about something that threatened me (usually in my teen years it had to do with failing a test). In those years, I had undetected reading problems. If I were in the school system now, I would be labeled as dyslexic. I would suffer agonizingly, hour after hour, to try to complete homework. The letters would jump. I would read the same sentence over and over. I used to have to take an index card, cut a window in the middle of it, and put it over the words to keep the letters from jumping. Anytime that I was asked something, that I was called on in class, fear would rush through my body and freeze it. I was unable to speak or to answer. Another F went down. However, if I would hear something or see it, it was like my brain just became an automatic tape recorder, and I would hold the image and be able to go back to it at any time.

What I wasn't aware of at the time was that I was engaged in more of a right brain activity, which triggers an alpha dimension, while most reading comes through a left brain activity, a beta dimension. I was not able to do this at the time. My end result for solving this problem was to keep my fears, to hide them, and to gloss them over by becoming the class clown. I would much rather take a failure for acting up in class—being sent out of the class, knowing that I made everybody else laugh—than to sit there with a blank piece of paper because I couldn't read the questions, since the fear would freeze my eyes and my mind as well.

I had great fun socially in grammar school and high school, but academically I suffered. I told no one. This affected me so much that by the time I was seventeen years old, I had a pinhole ulcer in my stomach. I would hide bottles of Mylanta in my night table drawer, wake up in the middle of the night in agonizing pain, and the only comfort was to chugalug from the bottle of chalk.

This pattern continued. One of my dearest friends would help me through the schoolwork. Even through college, one of my dearest friends would help me by reading to me, and then I would simply explain what she read. We both attended the same college, although I was rejected several times before actually getting accepted. The only reason why I was finally accepted is because I literally went to the admissions office with a check and said, "Here, take this; consider it my rent from September to December. If I don't make the grade, you can kick me out." I guess it was such an unorthodox approach that they didn't know what to do with me, and with a cashier's check on their desk, what could they do? So my dear friend continued to read to me all through college, and from that point I was able to just barely get by.

When I finished college, I became a high-school English teacher. I applied in the Newark, New Jersey, school area. I wanted to go there because I felt that the teaching would be more vital. I obtained a teaching position in Barringer High School in Newark. I felt at home. Perhaps it was because we all seemed to have the same learning problems. It was from this that I learned that anybody can learn. It is simply a matter of releasing the capacity from within to do it.

I was teaching for a few years when I finally decided it was time for me to get out on my own, so I moved from my family's home and set up an apartment with a friend. This change so distorted the images of safety in my brain that I developed severe panic and anxiety attacks. I would hyperventilate while driving. I remember one day when I was driving around a highway circle to cross over the highway and I began to experience a panic attack, thinking I was not able to get off the circle and properly exit from the road. This image so impressed me that I literally drove around the circle for ten minutes. I was frozen. My hands were white-knuckled around the steering wheel. I was sweating. My clothes were soaked in my own perspiration. After I finally did exit, I pulled to the side of the road and burst into tears. How could I continue? How could I go through life like this, always hiding? No one knew that I would experience such pain. It gripped at me. I danced with the demon in doorways, on highways, with others, alone. There was never a time that I didn't have the image in my mind that at any moment this feeling could just overcome me, take me.

These panic disorders got worse, until I finally developed a migraine headache that lasted three weeks. I was nauseous, vomiting until I had the dry heaves. I was gray. I couldn't eat or sleep. Nothing worked to get rid of the pain. I would cry at night, with my fist in my mouth so I would not wake up the adjoining apartment dwellers. This was in the summer of '75.

Finally, another friend came to me and said, "You have to get out. Let's get some fresh air. Try to walk around." Well, we were not out more than ten or fifteen minutes when a thought occurred. I said to her, "I want you to take me somewhere." "Where?" she asked, at this point figuring it must be an insane asylum. I said, "I want you to take me to see a teacher that I had in high school." She drove me there without question, figuring I'm either going to have some religious experience or lose my mind altogether.

I wanted to see a teacher—a nun, Sr. Joanne Ryan—whom I had had in high school. She was very helpful for me. She was the only one who really knew what I was going through all through high school, and when she would see me she would give me small words of encouragement that were hugely uplifting. She would smile at me and say, "Someday you're going to see the potential that you are." She believed in me in a way that I never thought I would ever see as a reality. And so, I went to visit her on that Saturday afternoon.

The meeting was brief—no more than thirty minutes, but in that thirty minutes she redirected the course of my life. She told me that she wanted me to take the Silva Method course. She said she had just taken it a few weeks or a month ago. I took it in full faith, not knowing what it was. She also taught me right then and there a breathing exercise. I laid flat on the floor, right in her office. She helped me to do the exercise by simply talking me through it. At the end of that meeting, we said our goodbyes. I told her I would take the program and let her know the results afterwards. Again, she reminded me that the potential within me was about to be found. Halfheartedly hearing this, I clutched onto the guidepost of "Take the Silva Method course." We continued to chat for a little bit. Again, I thanked her for her concern and belief in me.

It took me another month to save the tuition fee for this program, which at the time was $175. I continued to practice during that time the little exercise that she taught me. In fact, within about an hour after the meeting with Sister Ryan, I already began to feel some relief from my headache. I continued to practice her exercise until the class began. Every day I just simply started to feel better. I started to focus on more positive images, a little at a time. I was continuing to teach at Barringer High School during this time, and so I would reinforce the breathing exercises and the repetition of affirmations during the day. In fact, one of my favorite things to do, especially at the height of some tension-, anxiety-, or stress-filled moments during the school day, was to recite and picture the words from Psalm 23. I kept imaging it: "The Lord is my shepherd. Nothing indeed shall I want." I held this close to me as best as I could. I continued to breathe in and feel the imagery. I continued, sometimes four, five, even six times a day. I simply felt stronger and better.

Eventually I repeated the course several times, went into a training program, and over the course of three years became an instructor. I have been involved teaching various programs like the Silva Method for more than twenty years now. Truly this was a course that redirected my life. It gave me an inward journey. It gave me the way to make all my dreams into realities. It gave me the way to break out of the chains and the confinement of the limited self and to totally embrace and feel free in the potential self, the true self.

The memories of my countless failures in school, social settings, career efforts, and more now serve as my strength. They have helped me to create my true self from the inside out. The power is within me, and what were once my stumbling blocks are now my stepping stones.

How You See It

Whenever I think of the word *fear*, what usually seems to follow is something of a limitation, a threat, something that confines me. In fact, what usually follows is some type of failure, a broken dream, a goal that is not yet realized, which will be thought about for a long time, always seeming to be closely within reach. To say it simply, when I would say I fear something, "I'm afraid," what usually followed was "I can't." Again, we see the pattern of incongruence. I want to do something (the desire), but I can't (my behavior). It is a conflict.

Most people live their lives having a dream that will remain unrealized. They will have fears on all levels that make them dim the light on their talents. Most people's fears are defined by themselves as being more of the reality than a true reality, which is whatever you perceive and believe you will achieve. In this last statement, there is nothing apparently positive or negative, but simply a formula that says, "If I think it's so, it's so." This is really how the brain and mind work.

If we again take the definition of *fear*, we see that it is the image that makes us falsely believe that what we are perceiving is the reality. *Fear is an image.* It's something I see in my mind. Because it directly affects my body—that is, I have physical responses—I then believe it to be real in my outer world. I believe it to be real in terms of my abilities, and so I become what I think, not what I want, not what I am truly capable of.

The fear image is so close to the body that because I think it, it haunts me. It can permeate every part of my being. It programs my inner self. It becomes like an automatic reflex. From this, a person begins to feel halved. The person feels divided in a limited, fearful, and threatened self and potential self. The battle continues.

These fears can begin at any time in life. They can begin when an innocent child runs out into the school playground to meet friends to play, and unexpectedly a neighborhood dog rushes out just to play with the children also, but as the child perceives this dog approaching, fear occurs. The child will feel threatened. There is an immediate visceral response. There will be a pounding of the heart. There will be a tension in muscles, a widening of the eyes, even a scream. At that moment, the brain has made a picture: Dog + fun + unexpected = threat. The brain works like this, through association. Whatever happens, simultaneously the brain will take in, like a bioplasmic computer, and actually code into the cells of the brain that we call *engrams*.[8] That scenario is now recorded in the brain and will remain there and stay with this child well into adulthood.

---

[8] How the brain works with images has been researched by Jose Silva, who began his work in 1944 and is now the chairman of the board for the international transformational organization called the Silva Method. The Silva Method is in almost every country around the world and has been studied by nearly fourteen million people. This program's main objective is to teach people how to release the potential within them by learning about the brain. See also the "Scale of Brain Evolution" chart on page 45.

Some symptoms of this come in later life, such as allergies to fur or feeling uneasy, not confident, as he/she goes into new experiences, even if they're going to be fun. Social gatherings could make this adult person very uneasy and, according to the level of fear that had been coded in at childhood, this person could actually develop some social inadequacies.

What It Really Is

Research shows that there are several brainwave frequencies. You may not know that your brain is not only on, but on at a more fine-tuned level. Even when we're asleep, the innate intelligence that runs through our bodies remains on. Consciousness is always on. What shifts is focus. There are four brainwave frequencies, which are illustrated in the "Scale of Brain Evolution" chart: a *beta* brainwave frequency, and *alpha*, *theta*, and *delta*. Every night when we go to sleep we move through all of the four brainwave frequencies naturally.

- The beta frequency is the frequency that the brain exhibits when the person is conscious and awake and is involved in physical activity. As the person begins to relax, typically by taking a few deep breaths just before going to sleep, the brain will slow down.

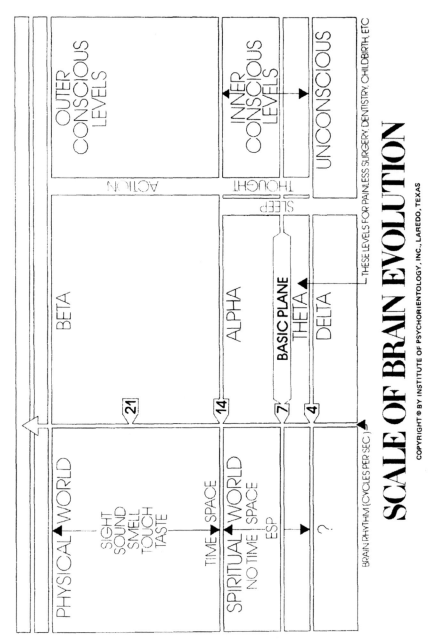

SCALE OF BRAIN EVOLUTION

COPYRIGHT © BY INSTITUTE OF PSYCHORIENTOLOGY, INC., LAREDO, TEXAS

Copyright 1969 by Institute of Psychorientology, Inc., and used by permission.

- The frequency now moves to an alpha brainwave frequency, slowing from fourteen cycles per second to about ten cycles per second.[9]
- This pattern will continue. It will decrease again into a theta and then to a delta. This happens in the first ninety minutes of sleep.
- At the end of this first ninety-minute cycle, the brain then shifts again and moves back to a theta and an alpha and will continue in this pattern, moving through alpha and theta throughout the night in ninety-minute intervals. These ninety-minute intervals are called sleep cycles, until the last ninety minutes of sleep when the brain exhibits only an alpha brainwave frequency.

What our research has proven is that at that alpha and theta brainwave frequency, the brain functions primarily to absorb imagery. It is the thought place. Notice how nature has given us two or three inner brainwave frequencies in which to do our thinking and one for action, beta. Most of us, however, don't even know that this is a function of the brain. The end result is the average person does all his or her thinking and acting perhaps mostly in the beta brainwave frequency. The difference between functioning at alpha and functioning at beta is awareness. In alpha, we function with a greater capacity. We function with a deeper sense of awareness. We function at the true vibration of human potential. It is at that inner level of the alpha dimension that the person is in touch with his or her true self. At that alpha dimension, ten cycles per second, the person is aware and has available to him or her the true natural energy source that we call the Inner Light, innate intelligence.

One common example of this alpha brainwave frequency and how it works to record images is the daydream. Research again

---

[9]   Jose Silva, *The Silva Mind Control Method* (New York: Simon & Schuster, 1977), 18-21.

shows that when we are daydreaming, we are actually changing the brainwave frequency from beta to alpha, and so nighttime dreaming and daytime dreaming have in common the ten-cycles-per-second vibration.

At alpha, we have been given the ability to think, to heal at a more rapid pace. This explains why, when we are not feeling well, there is a tendency to want to sleep and rest more, why rest for the body is one of our primary needs, for during the rest state, which is the alpha dimension, the body can rejuvenate at a faster rate—in fact, faster than at any other brainwave frequency. At the alpha dimension, we have the ability of keen perception because this ten cycles per second is the core connection to human potential. We have more information available to us at the alpha dimension than the beta, and so when we simply learn to turn on alpha, regardless of whether it is day or night, we are then able to tap into our true selves, our true power, our true ability to see through a situation clearly. We can make decisions that will give more positive results because more information is available to us. When we make a decision from the alpha dimension, it is key that the decision be positive, for whatever is sensed or visualized at this ten-cycles-per-second phenomena, be it positive or negative, the brain automatically records, and so here is where we become programmed. At the alpha-theta levels of brainwave frequency, our brains function again much like a computer. It is the bioplasmic computer enabling us to store all kinds of information to make life convenient and efficient. However, with lack of knowledge of how this bioplasmic computer works, all we store is fears, limitations, and the deep belief that we will remain vulnerable.

An example of how this alpha dimension can record is the ordinary experience of awakening with a radio on. We're still in a drowsy state. We are still exhibiting high vibrations of the alpha frequency, probably about ten or eleven or twelve cycles per second. We're in that dreamy state, still in bed, and we hear a song on the radio. Then finally we stir from our sleep, awaken, and go about our business. Perhaps later in that same morning we will begin to sing in our heads all the words of the song. The words are available because they have been recorded merely by listening to them in that dreamy state prior to full-awakened consciousness.

If words of a song can be remembered without us knowing it, think how strong programming can be from early childhood, since the brain functions about 75 percent of the time at the alpha brainwave frequency until the age of seven or eight. This is why that age is called the *age of reason*.[10] At that time, the brain begins to function with more full hemispheric potential, meaning that there is a true coordination between the right brain and the left brain, and so at this age of reason the child can then discern, begin to make choices of right and wrong, of what he or she chooses from an internal brain vibration capacity. Until that time, even as far back as in utero, whatever is thought of, felt, experienced, seen, or simply heard is written directly onto the engrams of the brain. The child is programmed.[11]

Look at the evidence here for healing of the inner child, where the child hears the parents violently arguing day after day and gets that coded into his or her brain. The child will then grow up with the feeling, the belief, that family is about violence. Without awareness, the child will inevitably repeat this pattern. The cycle will go on. Perhaps this is the key to release the doors of generations and generations of abuse, alcoholism, substance abuse. More and more research is pointing in that direction.[12]

---

[10] Jose Silva, *The Silva Method Manual* (Laredo, TX: Institute of Psychorientology, 1969), 9-11.

[11] Ibid., 9-11.

[12] For further reading, see Jose Silva, *The Silva Mind Control Method* (New York: Simon & Schuster, 1977); Norman Cousins, *The Celebration of Life* (New York: Bantam, 1991); Stanislav Grof, M.D., *Holotropic Mind* (New York: Harper Collins, 1990); Joan Borysenko, Ph.D., *Fire in the Soul* (New York: Warner, 1993); and Robert Stone, Ph.D., *The Secret Life of Your Cells* (West Chester, PA: Whitford Press, 1989).

From this construction of knowing about the inner potential of the self using an alpha dimension, as opposed to remaining only limited from a beta level of consciousness, it's easy to see how the split between the limited self and the potential self will continue unless the person consciously learns how to reprogram. This is the core of creating for a congruent personality. This is the portal for the person to turn every dream into a reality. This perhaps is the link between much of the scientific research that is now being explored and the statement made thousands of years ago: "Seek first the kingdom of heaven and all else shall be given to you. Know that the kingdom is within." Is the kingdom within a brainwave frequency? If the Creator sculpted such a unique work of art in the human being, breathing in full-power capacity into it, why couldn't it be then that by merely learning to change levels of awareness, which has now been proven by science, people could change any fear into a victory, drawing them closer to who they really are?

Let's explore for a moment the limited self. The limited self comes from limiting thoughts that get programmed at the alpha dimension. The effect, however, is on the physical body. Once I have a thought in my mind that says, "I can't," the first reaction is to my body. Again this is because the image began in the brain, moves through the whole nervous system, and the whole thought codes my every cell. I feel the fear. In feeling the fear, I make it so. I believe it. My eyes now do not see the truth. My eyes see the image that is written on every cell of my body, making it look as though this were the truth.

It doesn't even matter what it is that I'm afraid of. I could be afraid of heights. If I see the picture in my mind, my body will already begin to have the experience as if I were walking on top of the Empire State Building in the observatory tower. If I am afraid to let anyone get too close to me emotionally, it may be because I came from a family where there was no touching, and I therefore think that distance between people is normal, and anything other than that is abnormal and therefore threatens me. Later on in life, when I meet someone and want to draw close to that person, I will become frightened that there is something wrong. As someone draws emotionally close to me, I will do everything in my power, quite unconsciously, to actually destroy this relationship because my model in the brain is where I come from. In what is typically known as the *fear of intimacy*, there is no emotional closeness.

The old expression, "First impressions are lasting," is the vital truth here. First impressions are simply first impressions. They need to get changed and adjusted as life goes on. The key to life is adaptation. If we do not adapt physically, emotionally, mentally, and spiritually, we become dinosaurs. How limiting it would be to be a dinosaur walking on the earth today. If your first impression in childhood was that the one who knows the most wins, such as "Knowledge is power," "Know as much as you can," there may be a tendency in your life to acquire a great amount of knowledge, to read, to become quite successful intellectually. But again there is an abyss between the head and the heart, and so when someone else either knows more than you or draws close to you, you will feel mentally threatened. You can become argumentative. You will be afraid to be wrong. You will be afraid that you are not perfect. You will have a fear of imperfection.

If my early impression of the Creator were fire and brimstone, that God will punish me, or that God and all religious understanding come from merely following rules of right and wrong, I will believe that my God is a police captain, and so I will always feel threatened that this power will come out of the heavens and strike me down if I dare do anything that is not following the letter of the law. This, too, can cause an enormous amount of guilt spiritually. I will be so frightened that I will die, I will become either a religious zealot, or I could just go the opposite way, figuring the flames of hell are leaping at me now and so I might as well just become an atheist.

The sum total of our human experiences—physically, emotionally, mentally, and spiritually—will remain subjected to the perception in which they were first impressed, unless the person has a way of releasing these erroneous images and replacing them with positive, constructive, and creative ones. This sounds like a monumental task, but the truth is it's as simple as breathing. Even the first exercise from chapter one is a beginning of turning on this power from within. Just the simple relaxation exercise of breathing in and breathing out and sensing positive images, healthy images, constructive images, begins to erode the frightened, limited impressions that have actually coded themselves onto engrams in the brain. Whenever we close our eyes and take a deep breath, there is a phenomenal change in the physiological and the neurological aspects of the body. A new image literally gets printed right over the old one. If the new one is positive, the old dissolves quickly. If the new one is negative, it will simply reinforce the old stored information that is already convincing you that you must stay in your limited and frightened self.

From this model, it's easy to see how most people are convinced that they are limited because they are not aware of this power from within. They stay limited in their behaviors, in their jobs, in academic achievements. They will remain in damaged relationships. It is likely they will have a propensity to keep even a limited body that will eventually become more wounded and sick. Literally, most of us believe that we are victims of circumstances, and in this we are living a slow death. Life and its true power is to be released in the moment; the point of power is in the present. At any time people can rewrite their scripts; they can change the limited perception of themselves to end the battle, to once and for all slay the demon of fear. It literally is a picture that I make in my mind. The true self is born with safety from the Creator. Your whole life is based on your breathing. In that breathing we add then a positive image, a strong and clear image of self. The brain records it, the body feels it, hence the behavior will follow. It is in this repetition that success and happiness and prosperity are promised.

Your Worksheet

This exercise can be recorded in your own voice on a tape recorder so that you can take it with you and use it at the office, at home, and any time. The best way to do this is every day, at least once a day if not more, according to your need. The effectiveness of this program dissolves the limited self on a regular and everyday basis, releasing your confident self, helping you to see the truth in situations because you have now broken the barrier from the inner to the outer consciousness levels. The more that you continue to use this exercise, you will truly come to see and believe that there is no failure except in the mind of one who continues to see only the picture of the self as being limited, trapped, confined. By using this technique, regardless of the situation or circumstance, you will be able to be inner directed so that all outer behaviors are based in confidence and in truth, enabling you then to create a good and positive personal reality.

Create an affirmation that is simple and direct and always in the positive tense, like: **"I am calm and confident."** Merely by repeating this over and over, the brain takes this image to heart, and your body soon exhibits the behavior. By repeating this, writing it several times during the day, what will happen is the key word *truth* will dissolve fear. *Truth* and *fear* cannot exist in the same sentence. It is important also to use the following as a regular daily meditation exercise. It will change the images of the limited self into your true power self. The following exercise is called "Relaxing in the Power Self."

- Allow your body to be in a comfortable position, in a position where you know that you'll be comfortable sitting for about the next ten minutes. The best position is to be sitting up where your back is supported. However, if you feel more comfortable to be lying down because of physical limitation, allow your head to be comfortably resting on a pillow. The reason why it is preferable to be sitting up is that we are programmed to go to sleep when we lie down. In this exercise, it is important that we remain awake while resting. The key here is not sleep, but to rest and change the imagery in the brain.

- Allow yourself to be in this comfortable position now. The first thing to do is to adjust your body. Move your arms and legs until they are comfortable and at peace, and then begin to breathe in slowly. Take several deep breaths. The most important is just to breathe slowly and in an easy and rhythmic manner. Breathe in and out, in and out, and while you are breathing in and out, silently hear, "Relax, relax, relax." Do this ten times. "Relax, relax, relax," breathing in and breathing out, and repeating "Relax, relax, relax," and then again taking a deep breath, "Relax."

- Then focus your awareness in the center of your chest and imagine that there is a golden light there. It can be the flicker of a candle. You can even become playful, childlike, and pretend that you swallowed sunshine. Feel it right in the center of your chest where you know your heart to be. Begin to feel the warmth, the soothing comfort permeating through your body. If this visualization seems unfamiliar or even uncomfortable, just imagine you're all dressed in yellow, a glistening, fluorescent yellow, a golden light, and then let this light soak into all the muscles and the bones, the nerve fibers. Feel it moving, circulating, calming. Feel the sunshine on your face, a golden light showering all over you, including your scalp, and relax.

- Let this light emanate from the very center of your heart, so that you truly have a sense that it's coming from the center of you and then radiating outward, and feel the light soothing, warming, comforting you. And then repeat,

47

The light within me creates the power me, the good me, the confident me, the calm me, the healthy me, the happy me, the successful me, the prosperous me. The light within me is the God within me, and it is good.

- An appropriate time is about ten minutes. Always end these picture power sessions by saying: "The power me is within me. The light that is within me is God and it is good."

Chapter Four

Release the Fear Now!

What Happened To Me

For me, pain was fear's storage bin. Its toxic residue was in the cells of my body, tightening muscles, weakening full nervous system function. The result was stress upon stress—or disease. Many nights I would wake up and grope in the dark, trying to find my way into the night table drawer, hoping to find the Mylanta bottle was not empty from the night before. I hid the ulcer, the pains, and the panic attacks longer than Jonah's wallowing in the belly of the whale.

I felt that every inch of my body was foreign and my enemy. Friends would call and we would do some things together, whenever I could find enough emotional glue to get me out the door! But the whole time I was out, I was numb from the neck down, feeling like my head was stuck in an invisible fishbowl. I told no one of these feelings. The only thing that kept me emotionally alive was Psalm 23.

I would repeat it over and over, line by line. I would picture every phrase: "The Lord is my shepherd—nothing indeed shall I want. He made me to lie down in green pastures." I would so project myself into these words that I actually felt I was in a green healing pasture. I would then relax, become quiet and peaceful. From this I later realized something: that no two things can occupy the same space at the same time. So, you're either tense or relaxed. By using more of the relaxed words, I became just that. The power of language is just that—powerful.

How You See It

Perhaps the biggest problem in dealing with fear is releasing the bodily reactions that occur from it. When fear strikes, the body is its first victim. It attacks the mind and through this, since the mind is everywhere in the body, the body becomes totally victimized. Here's where lots of the phobic behaviors develop into lifetime trends and patterns. In these trends and patterns, people often focus on the phobic conditions that reside in the body rather than on the cause that came from the mind. This is because the power that fear has over the body can be so overwhelming that the need for relief is prominent. People seek relief from the choking feeling, the pain in the pit of their stomach that keeps them from eating properly or digesting their food, problems with muscle spasms and panic attacks, even resulting in even asthmatic attacks.

Because the body is so victimized by these conditions of fear, oftentimes fearful, frightened people are stuck resorting to medication or any way possible of simply relieving the pressure, the pain that they feel in their bodies. This is all they focus on for their relief, however temporary. For the fear can strike again, just like crabgrass continues to grow even though it's been mowed and it looks like it is gone. The problem is that the seed is invisibly rooted in the mind, but this energy of the mind permeates every cell of the body and captures every cell as its victim, keeping the whole body and the whole person trapped, imprisoned in the jail of fear.

What It Really Is

With this in mind, it is most important to seek immediate help from the pain of fear. Before explaining some very important techniques for releasing that fear in the mind, in the now, which will then free up the body from the pain of the fear, let's look at what the ego does.[13]

If we think of the ego as the unsafe you, then the ego is you thinking of yourself in any way that is limiting you: not smart enough, not attractive enough, not wealthy enough, not healthy enough, not tall enough, not capable enough. The ego then is the you that is simply not enough.

In this limited self, this is what the ego does. The minute you lose focus—when your consciousness swings back into a past where you were a victim, where you were not safe, where you were threatened, where circumstances overcame you, or you're thrown into the future where you have no control—in this single second, the ego preys upon you and forces you to live in finite time, thinking of yourself, your total being, as being part of a yesterday, a today, and a tomorrow. It begins to torment you and tell you such things as: "Don't you remember what happened to you the last time? How do you have any guarantee this won't happen again? Look at what happened every time that you sought to go forward and do this or do that, or you tried to establish for yourself some credibility, a positive relationship."

It keeps you either plugged in to the pain and guilt of the past or the worry and anxiety of the future. Thoughts run across your mind that make you feel frozen in the moment rather than fluid and joyful. In this feeling, in that single moment in the single feeling, the limited self, the ego, has attached itself like a parasite to every cell of your body. The result is some kind of physical reaction and sometimes even pain. The body then becomes the platform for this trickery.

---

[13] When I use the term *ego*, I am using it in the sense as it is stated in *A Course in Miracles*. Here, the ego is defined as the limited self, the self that can be threatened, that can be sick, that can be overcome, that can be conquered. The ego is the false sense of self that says you are finite and vulnerable to a world around you, to circumstances, places, persons and things.

The ego, making you think it's a real threat because now your body is really reacting, convinces you. When every cell of your body is responding in this frightened manner, your reality is distorted. You in turn believe the distorted reality because you can't breathe, you can't speak. There's tightness in the muscles of the chest. You're not able to speak, to act, to behave in ways that your real, higher mind wants you to. Because your body looks like it is frozen in fear, you believe this illusion to be the truth. In this moment, the ego (or the limited self) has won over, and conquered you because it got every cell to stay trapped in this time line of your life—nothing more than some yesterdays, some todays, and some tomorrows. Trapped in this time capsule, there is no escape from pain. You merely have to seek temporary comfort.

Here is where it is most important to understand the true self, the self as you were created, is the divine self. The divine self is not trapped in a time-space dimension. The divine self actually lives in eternity a moment at a time. It is freed up of the confines, the jail, of some yesterdays and some todays and some tomorrows. It is the finite self that is in constant battle with this infinite or divine self that causes all confusion and pain in a person's life.

To me, that's the micro. The unfortunate macro world outside us is this conflict of the finite self and the divine self projecting its battle on the world, including conflicts of racial discrimination, political unrest, economic problems, to name a few. It is perception of one's self that creates projection onto the world.[14] We then see the world as we see ourselves, not knowing that the view we have of our world is exactly equal to the view we have of ourselves. Once again, the ego thinks it has claimed a victory. Quite on the contrary, what is true is always true. "Truth needs no defense."[15] Awareness frees the divine

---

[14] Foundation for Inner Peace, *A Course In Miracles* (Farmingdale, NY: Coleman, 1975), I:35-41.

[15] Foundation for Inner Peace, *A Course in Miracles*, 2:77.

self and dissolves the finite self. The divine self is your true self, the one that God created. Here no opinion stands equal to you except the truth that you are as God has created you. You always were and you always will be, and the illusions of your mind have locked you in a body and captured you because of fear, one cell at a time, into some form of pain.

What we call miracles in life is simply the freedom of the inner self, the divine self, dissolving the illusion of the finite self. Chapter 1 of *A Course in Miracles* lists fifty principles of miracles. Some of these principles directly apply to this discussion here. They are principles 22, 23, and 26:

> Principle 22. Miracles are associated with fear only because of the belief that darkness can hide. You believe that what your physical eyes cannot see does not exist. This leads to a denial of spiritual self.

> Principle 23. Miracles rearrange perception and place all levels in true perspective. This is healing because sickness comes from confusing these levels.

> Principle 26. Miracles represent freedom from fear. Atoning means undoing. The undoing of fear is an essential part of the atonement value of miracles.[16]

These principles are often seen as, in fact, universal laws for the true spiritual self to emerge into a new way of looking at life in terms of time and space, and that is when one clearly accepts that one is a divine self—in fact, a light in a body, an endless being in a body. This endless being is free to make choices, choosing love or fear; in a single moment this being can release what seems to be fear

---

[16] Foundation for Inner Peace, *A Course in Miracles*, 1:2.

and darkness and dissolve it throughout the body and throughout its perception of its larger body, meaning its life, its environment, and ultimately the globe.

Whenever we reach into ourselves, into the true self, the divine self, the self that is made of pure light, the self that remains perfect as you are created, and we begin to accept that goodness and that beauty and that power, we then begin to use clear, positive, affirming statements such as, "I am the truth I see coming from the God within me." Our whole perception is changed and it is as if we have put on truth from the inside out, and therefore every cell is now seeing through the eyes of this truth.

This battle of the finite trapped-in-time me and the divine me that moves through all eternity in a co-creating relationship with God causes what I consider a type of double exposure on perception. I call it a *psychological cataract*. It is layers and veils of illusion over my eyes, meaning *e-y-e* (my eyes) and the pronoun *I* (my ego), that fools me, tricks me into seeing something that truly is not there. This *psychological cataract syndrome* is the cause of the bodily reactions of pain and discomfort, tension, anxiety, panic disorders in a body.

Using these theories we can, in fact, directly see immediate release of the fear in the body. Since the power in my body is not bound by time or space, but merely follows my direction, I can release every cell simultaneously from it. The following technique can be used to release the pain of the fear immediately. It is a visual and creative technique.

Your Worksheet A

The first step is to identify where in the body you feel the pain, discomfort, or tension, such as, "I feel it in my head, my neck, my throat, my chest, my abdomen, my back." You identify the parts of the body that are in the immediate pain caused by the fear. The second step is—in your mind, with your eyes closed, sitting in a comfortable chair—to picture the place in your body that hurts from the fear, that's frozen in the fear. Let's say, for example, it is tension in the back of the neck and across the shoulders.

- Picture the area and then, with an imaginary laser crayon, draw an outline totally encapsulating the area where the fear has lodged itself, forming discomfort and pain.
- Give it an object description, such as, "It feels as tight as a rope." Then focus on the rope. You've now objectified the pain. It is not a pain in the neck, in the shoulders, in the body. It is your mind looking at a rope.
- Then move your mind to the next step of visualization that says you are now imagining you're sitting looking at a video screen and you're looking at a rope. You would then see the encapsulated white line around the rope. You would then begin to describe to yourself, with eyes still closed, in detail what this rope looks like—its dimensions, its color, its texture, such as: The rope is eighteen inches long; it has five knots in it; the rope is about an inch in diameter; it's like a burlap; it's thick and bristly; it's heavy.
- Reduce the size of the rope, in the same way as you'd count from one to three: One, two, three; now the rope is twelve inches and has four knots. This would continue: One, two, three; it is now six inches and has three knots. One, two, three; now, it is three inches long and has only two knots. Then extend your hand and imagine that this rope has been reduced to an inch, enough to fit in your hand. Some people will describe pains as being stuck behind a wall of bricks. They reduce it to a tiny brick of an inch that they can hold in their hands. They are trapped in a vault. They reduce it to a tiny hunk of metal that's only an inch. So, in the last stage the object becomes only one inch, able to be held in the person's hand.

- You are now objectively holding out your hand and holding the remaining imaginary one-inch rope with one knot left in it in your hand. Again, one, two, three, and you sense it in your hand. Then look at it and at the count of three it turns into an ounce of glitter or sparkles or light, and you count again, one, two and three. Hold the glitter in your hands and then objectively press your hand to your chest, and when your hand touches your chest, you imagine that this one inch of sparkles or glitter or light enters back into your body as a healing.

This changes the image of fear into love. This also puts the energy back into the body, releasing every cell to be free again to be light. Regardless of what your original metaphor picture for the fear is, it always ends up to be an inch small and then changes into one ounce of glitter or sparkle or just simply a ball of light that gets pressed back into the body.

- Repeat this affirmation ten times:

I see the truth that is in me; the truth within me is God.

Repeat this statement ten times slowly, taking a deep breath, inhaling and exhaling with each affirmation. This alerts the inner consciousness to its truthful self once again. The ego lies dead, gone and vanished. All light dispels darkness. This sentence has been told several times. This is the actual visualization technique to do it.

The problem with fear is that it is a power struggle and we always need to have a way of using the power in the here and now. Whenever we're frightened, in that single moment the ego has temporarily convinced us that we are powerless, and so it is a power struggle then of the unimportant, insignificant me stuck in a world that's so big and vast versus the eternal me as God has created me, perfect in his eyes, because of his signature upon my soul, and from this I change in my decision making, I change in my thinking and in my behaviors.

Immediately repeat this technique whenever the feeling of fear occurs, which sometimes means you may have to stop what you're doing and go into another room—even if it's at work, excuse yourself and go into a restroom and sit and quietly go through this exercise. When you address it in the here and now, you resolve and release the fear right now. You actually retrain the brain to think of its true self as it has been designed—that is, the real power you, not the weak, victim you.

The more you put it off and say, "I'll do it when I get home; I'll try to address this later," the more that you're giving free reign and fuel for the ego to feed upon; it becomes parasitic. The fear uses those images like a parasite, sucking all the life and energy out of you, and then again trapping you into only staying with, "I'll do anything to release this feeling of fear and anxiety." It is most important, then, to have this exercise perhaps written out and placed in your wallet or purse, at work, in the office, somewhere where you can reach to it immediately and use it.

Another maintenance antidote is to use this following meditation on a regular basis. This will also retrain the mind to think of you in its true self, and that is your divine self. You will not be trapped in the fear of the moment, but rather you will be free in the here and now, living in God's love through all eternity, beginning one moment at a time. This begins to establish a completely different relationship with your inner self, enabling you to see clearly through all situations. Again, it is stressed that these exercises must be done on a regular basis.

Here I can think of my own life and my own fear traps so easily, where I literally became locked in my body; in my mind's eye I saw nothing but my frozen emptiness. I saw myself in the middle of all the anxiety attacks as a mere insignificant dot, not able to think straight, never being bright enough, intelligent enough, never being quite enough of anything. Little did I know that what I used as my remedy was actually a clear stroke of creative visualization genius.

I used to picture at those moments that the power of God was wrapping itself around me in light, protecting me in ways I couldn't protect myself. Even at times when I didn't feel the power of God, I kept saying it: "The power of God wraps itself around me and through me, protecting me." I would say this over and over. Many times I was caught in my car with anxiety attacks, and I would say it out loud with tears streaming down my face, and I would breathe deeply as much as I could, and it would dissolve. I would get to the next place. I would get to the next function of my life in that day—a little weary from the strain, but I'd get there, and then it would get less and less and less.

I always tried to keep a copy of Psalm 23 with me in all situations. Sometimes even not being afraid, I'd feel it in my pocket and know that the words on that paper were true, and it would give me the peace for which I so sought. I did this repeatedly for several weeks, months. The time is really insignificant, because one day I recognized that I had gone several days, a week, several weeks without a panic attack. The feeling was so natural to just be peaceful that I didn't even notice it. This is when I knew that the power of God is real and breathes with me, but I must choose to use it. I must choose to announce it, to name it, and claim it.

I got great strength in this and continued to repeat it in all situations, even before I was afraid. In fact, I didn't wait to get afraid. I simply did it as a natural course of events. I would wrap myself in the light and I'd feel that presence and that power. I would sometimes, even as I would drift into sleep, imagine light wrapping around me and around the bed and throughout the room. I'd picture, even as I was feeling sunshine on my face, that those were rays from God's own heart reaching out to touch me and to care and to tell me that I was okay. Whether this was imagined or real, the truth about it is it works because the power of God is real and works. But the lesson here is we must vote on it, choose it, and not neglect it. We must understand its reverence, its power, and its gentleness, and let it embrace us. This begins the process of peace.

Your Worksheet B

The following exercise is a maintenance meditation for releasing the body from any of its constrictions of fear. This exercise can be written out and taken with you, or even recorded into your own personal cassette, so that it can be used during the day. It must be a repetitious reinforcement, since we are prone in this distracting world to thinking ourselves vulnerable. To live as you were created is a commitment, to dissolve fear and see the truth that is you.

- Allow yourself to get comfortable. Lay flat on the floor or sit in a chair, undisturbed for at least ten minutes. If you have to, take the phone off the hook or put a Do Not Disturb sign on the door.
- Then you begin to breathe in and breathe out in a rhythmic manner, taking your time breathing in and breathing out. Picture a green light in the center of your chest, an emerald green with little flicks of silver and gold. You can even bring back some images to your mind to help you create this color, such as looking at a basket of emerald jewels, looking at an emerald city, an emerald gown, an emerald garment, that you're dressed in an emerald garment—anything that will help you to sense this color green, and then continue to let it radiate from the center of your chest until, in fact, you are all dressed in the green of the emeralds. Let it glisten. This is an ethereal light, so even you can imagine that there's a laser light of emerald green from inside your heart that's radiating

through your body, all the way down your legs into your toes, all the way up your back and chest, across the back of your neck and shoulders and down your arms and fingertips, washing over your scalp and face.

- Then you would begin to repeat the affirmation ten times. Once you see yourself completely in the green, you say the affirmation ten times:

  I see the truth in me; the truth in me is God.

Over and over:

  I see the truth in me; the truth in me is God.

- Continue to say this slowly until you reach the count of ten. Then take your time and allow a white light to enter at the top of the head, at the crown of the scalp, picturing that this white light is connected to the very center of the universe, somewhere in the middle of the sky, like an umbilical cord, a silvery light umbilical cord that moves through the center of your scalp and now cleanses any shade of darkness, anxiety. Continue to move the white light. This is a white light of search, a searchlight that moves through your body searching for fear anywhere in the caverns of your muscles, the walls of your muscles, the bones, the nerve endings, searches it out and dissolves it, and so your lasting, remaining image is simply of you in luminous white that now is inside out all the way down to your toes. Continue to do this on a regular and everyday basis and it will continue to keep dissolving the illusions of fear.
- The end of this exercise is simply to repeat now ten times:

  I am beginning to see the light in me and the light is good, the light is peace, the light is God.

Part II

Transition

Chapter Five

Guilt—the Hidden Agenda

What Happened To Me

Through all the years of fear, what I feared most was that a belief or opinion of myself just might be true. What if I'm really not important, not really good? What if there's something wrong with me?

These feelings were apparent when I was teaching in Barringer High School. I really loved the kids. I could relate to their insecurities. I paid attention first of all to their issues of self-esteem and secondly to the English curriculum. I had to; it was their first need. I loved every day of it. But initially I wasn't tenured, so the fear of losing my job was a constant threat. At that time an exam was necessary for qualification of permanency. My dear friend Vicki, also the department chairperson, offered to help me prepare for the test. She insightfully knew of my hidden fears. In fact, Vicki was the single person who unconditionally loved me and my true teaching abilities. Many times she would say, "You are a great teacher, with a pure heart; you just don't know it yet."

So Vicki would stay with me after school to go over some old tests. I would freeze up so badly that I wouldn't even be able to speak. I'd just sit there with a vacant stare. With every question she'd ask,

I'd withdraw more. Finally, one afternoon, I just broke down and sobbed. Vicki stayed calm and just kept reminding me of my true abilities.

Ironically, I never even had to take the test! Shortly after that, the district changed policies and I became tenured anyway.

How You See It

What is so powerful and blinding about fear is that it seems to act upon us. It seems as if something just overtakes us, like an involuntary muscle. It can strike at any time. Whenever it does hit, it seems that it may or may not have something to do with the present. In fact, as the person is going through some type of anxiety attack or panic attack, it seems totally irrational and illogical to bystanders. Meanwhile, the person suffering from the fear is riveted in a frozen ice block of his or her own thoughts and feelings that are a true indication to him or her at the moment that there is something to be afraid of, there is something threatening that's going on.

Right there, in that example, we can see a contradiction. The person experiencing the fear thinks there is something real to be afraid of, while the person not experiencing the fear has a different perception. With this contradiction, we can begin to peel away at the fact that all fear is rooted in one cause: perception. What is it that is going on in the mind? What is it that's going on in the mind's camera eye that makes that person feel that there is something that might threaten or weaken him or her or cause some condition of unsafety?

What It Really Is

As we peel away deeper, we can see that in the moment of fear there is a contradiction, not only in the perception of those experiencing fear versus those not experiencing fear, but also a conflict in time referencing. Those who are experiencing the fear see something that is not presently in front of them, but rather perceive something that may be threatening based on some prior past experience. What they are actually doing is bringing up a picture from the past. They are in that moment reliving that past. Whatever happened in the past, their limited perception and opinion of that circumstance made them believe that they were in a weakened, vulnerable, victimizing set of circumstances and situations. Whatever that event was, the dynamics of it simply dissolved. What remains and lingers is a haunting refrain of that incident, and that there is something powerless in them that actually allowed the threat from the outside to permeate them on the inside, causing some sort of pain, discomfort, failure, or loss.

The psyche interprets this powerlessness as rooted in the fact that the person experiencing the fear literally has no value, and so the conflict, then, is in the person fighting, "Am I a person of value and power?" or "Am I not a person of value and power?" Because something happened that made that person feel vulnerable, regardless of whether it was a physical, emotional, or mental threat, the lingering scar remains. "This must have happened to me because there's something defective in me." This is what the psyche of the frightened person says. This feeling of insignificance, this feeling of wrongdoing, this feeling of not having any power over the outside world convinced the person that it was because there's something wrong with him or her. These people think they're not smart enough, strong enough, intelligent enough, pretty enough, rich enough. They don't communicate well enough. They're not attractive enough. Whatever it is that they are not enough of, these fearful persons believe that this lack is because they are actually damaged goods, if you will, from the beginning. They think that there's something wrong with them. "Otherwise, why would I have attracted this situation, these abusive parents, this alcoholic relationship, these bad grades, this bad relationship, these painful experiences?" What remains is just the memory of the belief that they are defective. As Gerald Jampolsky puts it:

> I'm never upset for the reason I think. Most of us have a belief system based on experiences from the past and on perceptions from the physical senses. Have you considered that what we believe is what we see or, as Flip Wilson put it, "What you see is what you get"? Because our physical senses appear to relay information from the outside world to our brain, we may believe that our state of mind is controlled entirely by the feedback we receive. This belief contributes to a sense of ourselves as separate entities who are largely isolated and feel alone in an uncaring and fragmented world. This can leave us with the impression that the world we see causes us to feel upset, depressed, anxious and fearful. Such a belief system presumes that the outside world is the cause and we are the effect.[17]

With this kind of a belief system, what the frightened person experiences is separation from power. The person believes power is on the outside and he or she is void of power, therefore void of value. Soon after this first impression seeps into the inner conscious state, the person assumes that this separation is, in fact, a separation from the author of power, meaning God. Even if the person has not a strong religious conviction, we all innately understand at some deep level that we did not create ourselves, and so when we feel the separateness, the aloneness, we feel detached, isolated from a source of goodness or power or protection, and these values are what are usually assumed to be the source of God. Those with religious conviction may more clearly identify that their separation is from God. They believe that

---

17   Gerald G. Jampolsky, M.D., *Love Is Letting Go of Fear* (Berkeley, CA: Celestial Arts, 1979), 71.

this separation from God is caused because of their unloving nature, their defectiveness, their poor quality as a person. They feel one of two things. They will feel "I am a defective model and therefore God doesn't really know me personally; I don't count; I'm insignificant," and therefore, they feel abandoned, detached, separated away from a life source that will ever become a wellspring for goodness, health and happiness. Or they will feel "I'm a defective model and I did wrong, so God will punish me for the wrongdoing. I will be judged and I will live in shame, hidden, isolated away from any of the good inheritance I might have had from God."

With these examples, we can see that way down deep under a fear, which is again a false perception or an illusion, there is one single cause. It's the hidden agenda—guilt. The actual cause of fear is guilt. We feel guilty because we assume out of false perceptions that these victimizing circumstances that occurred in our life that produced the fear feelings happened because of something we did or because of something we are, and in both cases we have assumed this is wrong and defective.

In his book, *The Art of Loving*, Erich Fromm states:

> The experience of separateness arouses anxiety. It is indeed the source of all anxiety. Being separated means being cut off, without any capacity to use my human powers. Hence, to be separate means to be helpless, unable to grasp the world, things and people actively. It means that the world can invade me without my ability to react. Thus, separateness is the source of intense anxiety. Beyond that, it arouses shame and the feeling of guilt. This experience of guilt and shame in separateness is expressed in the Biblical story of Adam and Eve. After Adam and Eve had eaten of the tree of knowledge of good and evil, after they had disobeyed, after they had become human by having emancipated themselves from the original animal

harmony with nature, after their birth as human beings, they saw that they were naked and they were ashamed. Should we assume that a myth as old and elementary as this has the prudish morals of nineteenth century outlook and that the important point the story wants to convey to us is the embarrassment that their genitals were visible? This can hardly be so, and by understanding the story in a Victorian spirit we miss the main point, which seems to be the following: After man and woman having become aware of themselves and of each other, they are aware of their separateness and of their differences insomuch as they belong to different sexes, but while recognizing their separateness they remain strangers because they have not learned to love each other. The awareness of human separation without reunion by love is the source of shame. It is, at the same time, the source of guilt and anxiety.[18]

Because of this hidden agenda, it is very difficult for frightened people to ever really see what causes them to be frightened. They will identify all the symptoms of the fear as the actual cause of the fear. They will call it being afraid of heights, being afraid of water, close spaces, flying; they are afraid of large animals; they are afraid of illness, catastrophes, and so forth. And all of these symptoms that they are naming as the real object of their fear really mask and serve to pull the consciousness off of the main root, which is guilt and shame. People secretly harbor this guilt and shame, thinking they must have done something to deserve this life circumstance; they must have somehow become such shameful people, either by deed or just by birth, that they should feel so separate and isolated from power and from life.

---

[18]   Erich Fromm, *The Art of Loving* (New York: Harper and Row, 1956), 7-8.

The main focus, then, of transformation in human development is to identify this guilt, to find where in the person's life, if possible, he or she assumed this guilt, and then to purge it by recognizing that it is a virtual impossibility to ever be separate from the power of God. The power of God is always and forever intricately placed through every breath we take into every cell in our body. This life force is a given. It is, then, as *A Course in Miracles* would describe it, totally insane to think of ourselves as guilty. This doesn't mean that we can live irresponsible and reckless lives without any mutual respect for others. In fact, it means the opposite. It means that you are totally responsible for all of your behaviors, for all of your actions, for all of your perceptions and decisions, and at the same time the quality and value of who you are cannot be altered. The who that you are is permanent; the what that you do is what will vary. Because we have shifted our perception and seen circumstance as cause rather than thinking and belief as cause, we get trapped in a vicious cycle of never being able to rectify any of the guilt or shame that we either have acquired or manifested in our own lives through our own thinking and acting. The transition in this reverse cycle happens when we understand the true nature of forgiveness. For in forgiveness, we peel off the illusion that we are insignificant and of no value, and rendered powerless and therefore separate from God. We see that the deeds and decisions we made were made out of a no-value self, and we then correct those decisions, we correct those behaviors, now based on a valued self. We correct the deed, knowing always that the doer is permanently one with God and will forever remain loved by God.

Jampolsky describes forgiveness in this manner:

> Forgiveness is the action of inner peace. Inner peace can
> be reached only when we practice forgiveness. Forgiveness
> is the letting go of the past and therefore the means for
> correcting our misperceptions. Our misperceptions can
> only be undone now and can be accomplished only through

letting go whatever we think other people have done to us or whatever we think we've done to them. Through this process of selective forgetting, we become free to embrace a present without the need to reenact our past. Through true forgiveness, we can stop the endless recycling of guilt and look upon ourselves and others with love. Forgiveness releases all thoughts that seem to separate us from each other. Without the belief in separation, we can accept our own healing and extend healing love to all those around us. Healing results from the thought of unity.[19]

Your Worksheet A

In this next exercise, we will focus on some circumstance or situation in the past that possibly allowed the misperception to etch in the haunting refrain of guilt and shame. In this exercise, you will be able to identify: Did you feel abandoned by God or did you feel ashamed in front of God? This will release the event that caused the guilt. This will begin the process of undoing the false perceptions about you as you have named them, the no-value you, into the real you, the powerful, valuable you as God has created you.

- Make yourself comfortable. You can be in a sitting position with eyes closed or lying down. It is preferable that you have a comfortable head and neck and back support to make sure that all muscles are comfortable and at ease. Begin, then, in this comfortable position and keep your eyes closed.
- Breathe in and out. Let this breathing become a little deeper and a little slower every time. Take your time, breathing in and breathing out. As you continue, let the breath of life that you're breathing now become a healing green light, like an

---

[19] Jampolsky, *Love Is Letting Go of Fear*, 35.

emerald green. Let it sparkle and glisten as you continue to breathe in and out, and as you are breathing in continue to repeat the word *relax* several times. This will encourage your sense of relaxation.

- At the count of three, you will allow a memory of the past to come to mind, some memory that was hurtful, painful, that angered you, depressed you, upset you, rendered you out of control in one way or another, where you felt totally powerless. You may only have a small piece of the memory at this time. However, you can repeat this exercise at any time so that you can have further clarification. Let whatever feeling or impression, any image, any symbol, just simply come to you. Just trust your instincts; trust your first impressions.

- One, two, three. Begin to focus on a feeling of being really upset somewhere in the past—an anger, a pain, a suffering, something that victimized you, something that made you feel totally insignificant and of no value, something that caused deep depression. Review this time in your life and ask yourself the questions: Whom did I believe? Where did I believe God was at that time? Did I believe that God abandoned me because of my insignificance and left me alone and separate, unable to handle the situation? Or did I believe that God would certainly punish me for the wrongdoing, for the shame? At that point, you covered your face, your eyes, from the truth about who you are. The burden of guilt lay heavy in your heart, and from that point on you hid behind a mask, thinking erroneously that you were not important, had no value, had no power in your life, and that the world was truly a dangerous place and you'd never be safe. Sooner or later, something else would happen and you'd be victimized again.

- Now begin to see yourself differently, to see yourself connected to the power of God. See that the beautiful emerald green light that is within you is pouring from the very heart of God, from the very center of the universe, and into you as a constant life force, feeding your body, your soul, your heart, and your mind with all that is good, with all that is truly honest and peaceful and filled with wisdom, and that at the moment this set of circumstances occurred, you did not see yourself as eternally connected to this power, but assumed incorrectly. You can choose differently now. You can correct the deed, knowing that that is a simple matter of re-seeing yourself as good.

- When I don't see myself as good, when I see myself as bad, I am most likely to make bad choices and bad decisions, but when I see myself as good and connected to the good one, I am more likely to choose good decisions and behaviors. Correct the deed now rooted in the goodness that is always you. Ask for forgiveness from those that you may have offended and forgive those who might have offended you. Regardless of how great or how small, it is only a matter of illusion that we strike out at each other because we do not know that we are forever in the arms of God, kept safe, directed, and protected. This is the truth.

- Begin the process of inner peace now by reclaiming your true identity. This may take some practice. Even if you continue slowly, day by day, taking ten or fifteen minutes a day to use this exercise, the truth will set you free. There will be no more shame, no more guilt, no more pain. What shall remain is you, just as God created you.

- When you are comfortable to do so, open your eyes. Respond in a journal, writing down thoughts or feelings that you can use to reflect upon at some later time. The truth cannot be altered in you, and the truth is that God breathes when you breathe.

When we can look at fear in this new way, knowing that it is rooted in guilt, and then truly address the guilt and see that even that is an illusion because it's based in an untruth, it's based in something that could never be, which is that I'm separate from God and therefore powerless, helpless, hopeless, when we can see this as the center root, the main cause of our fear, we begin in the single moment to resurrect out of our hell of fear. The demon is powerless at last.

Again, in *A Course in Miracles*, it is explained:

> Fear is always a sign of strain arising whenever what you want conflicts with what you do. This situation arises in two ways. First you can choose to do conflicting things, either simultaneously or successively. This produces conflicted behavior which is intolerable to you because the part of the mind that wants to do something else is outraged. Second, you can behave as you think you should but without entirely wanting to do so. This produces consistent behavior but entails great strain. In both cases, the mind and the behavior are out of accord, resulting in a situation in which you are doing what you do not wholly want to do. This arouses a sense of coercion that usually produces rage. A projection is likely to follow. Whenever there is fear, it is because you have not made up your mind. Your mind is therefore split and your behavior inevitably becomes erratic. Correcting at the behavioral level can shift the error from the first to the second type, but will not obliterate the fear. It is possible to reach a state in which you bring your mind under my guidance without conscious effort, but this implies a willingness that you have not developed yet. The Holy Spirit cannot ask more than you are willing to do. The strength to do comes from

your undivided decision. There is no strain in doing God's will as soon as you recognize that it is also your own. The lesson here is quite simple, but particularly likely to be overlooked. I will therefore repeat it, urging you to listen: "Only your mind can produce fear."[20]

The steps of atonement are also stated in *A Course in Miracles*, further on in that same passage. They are listed as:

- Know first that this is fear.
- Fear arises from lack of love.
- The remedy for a lack of love is perfect love.
- Perfect love is atonement.

In this way, we see forgiveness as the link to the miracle. Miracles are the re-establishing of order in all levels of the human being, physically, emotionally, mentally, and spiritually. Wherever there is disorder or chaos, or even disease, it is from a lack of the true perception of who we are. Hidden in each person is some guilt, some shame. It is the hidden agenda that is causing the ongoing, frightening suffering of our globe. This transition of reaching in, purging the guilt, then rising above, is the main focus of transition in each person's life. We will name these transitions *miracles*. The miracle is simply what is natural to you, and that is that you live at an optimum, that you live with the full expression of God's power moving through you.

In a later chapter, *A Course in Miracles* offers the following:

The miracle does nothing. All it does is to undo, and thus it cancels out the interference to what has been done. It

---

[20] Foundation for Inner Peace, *A Course in Miracles* (Farmingdale, NY: Coleman, 1975), 1:25.

does not add. It merely takes away, and what it takes away is long since gone, but being kept in the memory appears to have immediate effects. This world was over long ago. The thoughts that made it are no longer in the mind, that thought of them and loved them for a little while. The miracle but shows the past is gone and what has truly gone has no effect. Remembering a cause can but produce illusions of its presence, not effects. All the effects of guilt are here no more, for the guilt is over.[21]

Because we are so used to living in guilt and in fear, frightened at the very core that at any moment something else could happen, it actually feels initially uncomfortable to be that free and to be that loved, and so even this takes practice. When we are peaceful from within, we welcome it upon the onset, and then, because of our habit of not trusting in what we see, we assume that this peace will fade. And so, again practice is needed here—practice and trust that inner peace is the only thing about you that can't be taken away because it belongs to God, and who is more powerful than the power one, the Author of Life?

In *A Course in Miracles*, volume III, the manual for teachers, again we are helped to understand that once the correction is made, it does last, but again it is our interpretation that varies, and truth becomes diminutive and meaningless. Correction has one answer to all of this and to the world that rests on this:

> You but mistake interpretation for the truth and you are wrong, but a mistake is not a sin nor has reality been taken from its throne by your mistake. God reigns forever and his laws alone prevail upon you and upon the world. His

---

21   Foundation for Inner Peace, *A Course in Miracles*, 1:547.

love remains the only thing there is. Fear is illusion, for you are like him.[22]

"In order to heal," says *A Course in Miracles*, "it thus becomes essential for the teacher, the example of God, to let his own mistakes be corrected."[23] What will keep this correction forever in our mind, what will continue to cleanse our perceptions, is to practice inner peace. It is the only goal of life: to establish and to remind ourselves that what is true about us is the fact that God is with us, that power is love, it is unconditional, it makes no judgment, it makes no assessments, no accountabilities of right and wrong, it holds each one of us in perfect light, and that the only thing that blocks us from this vision is a false belief that we have been abandoned or we have something to be ashamed of. Out of this guilt is born fear.

Your Worksheet B

In this next exercise we can learn to practice inner peace on a regular and daily basis so that it becomes our single focus every day, so that when we enter into our daily activities we can begin with peace and bring it to the world, making more people alert to the true self that they are, merely by our example.

Practice and write this affirmation over and over, and the result will be the peeling off of the layers of shame and guilt that you, through misconception, have placed upon the true you.

- Allow yourself to be in a comfortable position, closing your eyes again. Let your body be in a position that is comfortable to remain in for a while. Begin to take a few deep breaths, breathing in and breathing out. Feel how good it is to

---

22   Foundation for Inner Peace, *A Course in Miracles*, 3:45.
23   Foundation for Inner Peace, *A Course in Miracles*, 3:19.

continue to breathe in and to breathe out, knowing that this breath of life is endless and it is perfect, and every breath you take carries with it full wisdom, full power, full healing, full goodness. This is who you are. You are this life, this breath of life. You are connected to it.

• Continue to relax, and as you continue to breathe, a little deeper and a little slower every time, let each breath now become a beautiful, radiant, white light, breathing it in and breathing it out. Really focus on your body. Begin at the scalp and allow the light to fill and permeate through every part: scalp and head and face; all the way to the back of the neck and the throat and shoulders and down the arms and fingertips; all the way down the spine and back; all the way through the chest, lungs, and abdomen; all the way down to the lower spine, hips, thighs, knees, calves, ankles, and feet. See only light in all parts of you, for this is who you are: perfect, shameless, and without guilt. For this light is a gift; it is God's presence in you that remains no matter what.

• Begin now to hear inside, from a still voice way deep in your heart, as if it was the voice of God and then know it is the voice of God, saying: "I am with you all days, even to the ends of the earth, and I love you, no matter what." Repeat this over and over, several times, and at the end simply say:

In this, o Lord, I can remain at peace.

Part III

Living in Love

Chapter Six

Being Me Without Shame

What Happened To Me

My shame and guilt became so fused that the thought of ever truly loving or being loved became more vague. Sure, I thought I loved many times in my life. But with time I saw that much of what I called love was really a repetition of a victim-rescuer cycle, of which I played both sides according to circumstance. No matter who it was that I was loving, there was always the shadow of a hole in my soul. It was a void of confusion caused by the unanswered question, What is my real worth? I began to search within to find answers. I wanted to know, "Do you know me, God, really, as a person, by name? Do you know me, love me for me?"

I continued my quest and found another great friend and teacher by the name of Fr. Albert Gorayeb. Father Al was a Byzantine Catholic priest and Silva instructor. In fact, he was my Silva Method instructor. We became colleagues when I became a Silva instructor in 1978. Father Albert truly was a great priest, teacher, and friend. He was a visionary. Anyone who knew him learned something, even if he or she didn't realize it at the time.

So here I was sitting in one of his lectures as he described how God created us. He said, "The full power of God is breathed into your flesh and as you breathe, God breathes. His power can never be taken from you."

With this, I began to picture that act of Creation. What I saw in my mind was an image of the Lord taking a breath of radiant light and breathing into me. In this I glowed in the same light. I felt warmth and peace. I felt God's love. I can still feel it now just by mentioning it. The Lord kisses us into existence with a love that remains forever. From this act of Creation real value is always given.

How You See It

Let's begin with just talking about the nature of love. What is the nature of love? Before I give a definition that I'd like to use as a kind of lens through which we will see a new perspective about who we are and what our power is, I want to separate it almost into a kind of team one and team two, or the home team versus the visiting team, to see where the conflict is. What usually happens when we talk about love is that we usually have some fixed ideas, expectations, feelings about it, dreams about it—what we think it ought to be and should be and should feel like. Then we drag it out further by claiming this is how my life ought to be, what it should look like. And then we have something called the "way it is," which is what we live with every day.

I'll start with *normal love*, and the normal comes from the definition of what *normal* means—average. When all of us are grouped together and tell our stories of love and life, then someone draws a graph or picture that represents those comments. This is a cluster of people's experiences. That's what *normal* means. *Natural* is going to have a completely different definition.

Normal love begins in the storybooks. It begins in the fairy tales.[24] It begins in setting up a conflict. Most fairy tales have a

---

[24]   Susan Forward, Ph.D., *Men Who Hate Women and the Women Who Love Them* (New York: Bantam, 1986), 19-20.

woman in some type of distress. She's the damsel in distress, and then what happens? The outside source (the knight in shining armor) will rescue her from this powerless position. She's safe. They ride off into a sunset. It's not "And they rode off the cliff." It's always "They rode off into the sunset" and then up comes THE END and the credits. That's the end of the story.

The problem with that is that's not what we really experience, but it sets up a protocol subconsciously from early on. It says that love is about conflict and love is about rescuing one person from another person or from some danger.[25] Some of us have read "Little Red Riding Hood." Talk about dysfunctional families; she goes to her grandmother's house and then she's eaten by a wolf. What it basically says is that love comes when you're in trouble and powerless, and it sets up one party not having the power and the other party having it. The other person makes the one in trouble feel better and get rescued, and then what? The end. It's finished. So now, let's see what we've done with this *normally*.

This creates an image that if I want love, I need to pick a side. Am I the victim or am I the rescuer? And I will go out and become one or the other. It sets up you have to either be a victim or you have to be a rescuer. It sets up that in order to get love, there's got to be a conflict. In order to get love—that's another problem. I have to get it. Love is something to go and get. "I'm going to get me some love. That's what I'm going to do. It's Saturday night. I'm going to get me some love." It sounds like to begin with you are in deprivation because you don't have it. This is the normal construct for love. Then what?

At the end of the "damsel in distress, here comes the knight in shining armor, ooh la la, Sassoon, I feel so much better," there is no room for growth or change, because there are only two clear dynamics for that relationship: a victim and a rescuer, the end. So

---

25   Michael L. Barnes and Robert J. Sternberg, *The Psychology of Love* (New Haven, CT: Yale University Press, 1988), 168-177.

to prevent a relationship on that model from ending, the people keep finding a new problem so that one party can be a victim and one party can be the rescuer. They literally start the story all over again and never get to the end; they just keep repeating it. These are people who are always in crisis in their relationships. There is always something going on: Somebody fell through a roof; the window came out; somebody's sick; we have no money; the chicken blew up in the oven. There is one crisis after another. "Where are the kids?" "I don't know; I left them in the dryer."

One crisis after another, and they are so very, very steeped in the subconscious model that they actually don't know it. They are totally unaware that this is what they are doing for the most part, because they've got this normal love definition imprinted in their brains, way in the back of their memory tanks. It's way back here from storybook land, which says this is what love is. So now they're adults, and in order for them to go and get it, they've got to be in conflict and continue the pattern of victim-rescuer; conflict, victim-rescuer; conflict, victim-rescuer.

If they don't want that love to die, because end also means finality or death—let's say two people love each other underneath but they don't have a natural definition for love, which we're going to get—they have to stay in the dynamics of the conflict to keep it alive. These people nitpick each other. They just keep it going and keep it going because in their heads is, "Once we resolve the conflict and there's no more conflict to be had, then what will we do? It's the end." The end of what? The end of love. Because for them, again, the definition of love is conflict and rescue. The circumstance in which love happens is the conflict and the two parties—one is victim, one is rescuer. One is victim, one is rescuer also means one is dominant and one is submissive. One's got the cookies and one doesn't. One's got the money; the other one doesn't. One's got the security; one doesn't. These are all to get filled in under normal love. This is in the back of our minds. This comes from us normally (again, it means "average") from an experiential conditioning, from the world of books and television. It's in there, subtly.

There's another normal love imprint that comes to us from our families.[26] The normal imprint that comes to us from our families is whatever the dynamics of our whole family were. That includes mother and father and siblings. It is not just you and your mother, you and your father. It is the dynamics of the family, however many there were: two, three, four, nine, plus the dog, cat, and canary. That whole unit made the impression that says this is the way people treat each other when they are loving. So if you came from a family of screamers, you screamed. And if you came from a family of "We don't talk about anything," if somebody was a talker and the best thing for you since sliced bread, you'd shy away from that person because it's not what you're used to. So again, there's an imprint. This is a normal imprint to the back of the brain, deep in long-term memory, that says, "Whatever my family went through and experienced in this thing called 'this is how we lived' is what I now think love is," and there's no way that this matches what you expect in your life right now. Do you see the conflict already? So, let's look at the family—the family definition of *love*.

If you came from a family of musicians, there would be a likelihood you would be born, even genetically, with a propensity for music.[27] Now, if you chose to play an instrument or sing or dance, fine. If you came from a family of lawyers, there would be a propensity within you to understand that, and so forth. It's an imprint that we're born with—it's now proven that this can be imprinted chromosomally,[28] that it passes through genetically from generation to generation,

26 Harville Hendrix, Ph.D., *Getting the Love You Want* (New York: Harper and Row, 1988), 17-22.

27 Deepak Chopra, M.D., *Ageless Body, Timeless Mind* (New York: Harmony Books, 1993), 22-24.

28 Chopra, *Ageless Body*, 22-26.

etched into our DNA. That's how much we can't escape it. So the family imprint in you is very strong and very subtle, because you don't remember when you weren't with your family, do you? First impressions are lasting.

Your first love is not your first attraction (that might have come in teen years or twenties). That's not your first love. Your first experience with love was the dynamics of your family and that's what got impressed, but nobody said to you, "Do you see what's going on here? This is normal love. It has nothing to do with nature, honey." You're going to figure it out after years of therapy, and probably a big bill. Now, in no way am I implying that everybody's family is to blame. In fact, it is my intention to say just the opposite as we go through from this side of the fence, which is normal love, and then get to the other side, which is natural love. It's absolutely my intention to clear up the blame game in love, because we have to get on with the joy of life. That's what this first discussion of what is the nature of love is serving.

So, we watched our mothers and fathers, and we watched how the woman acted, how the man acted, how the man and woman interacted. Then the pattern was duplicated from our favorite parent, or the dominant parent—the one whom we liked a lot or the one who dominated. Domination doesn't mean you like them. You could love and like your parents differently, and it's the dominant, or again the more-liked parent, the one whom you'd seem to favor or imitate or resemble or model. Oftentimes, you will then repeat that parent's life. So if you were modeling after your mother—this is very old information,[29] but we're going to see it take a new turn—there's a likelihood you're going to choose your father. If you modeled after your father, there's a likelihood you're going to choose like your father did and choose somebody who's like your mother. No matter who you

---

[29]   Seymour Feshbach and Bernard Weiner, *Personality* (Lexington, MA: D. C. Heath, 1986), 146-147.

are, the girl child or the boy child, you will absolutely repeat in your life both parents in relationships. We will all choose our parents. You may choose a person who is a combination of the two, according to circumstance and situation. Sometimes you'll see this person acting and communicating to you and repeating the same dynamics as what you had with that parent, and sometimes it's the opposite parent, and you will also find that you sometimes are both parents. We will always repeat finding our parents in our relationships, and we will always repeat acting out love as if we were our parents. Always. Why? Because first impressions are lasting and it was your first jump start in getting out in the world and learning about love. So this normal love is a combination of things we heard from society and stories and television, what we learned in school and from teachers, and it is also a combination of our parents.[30]

What you're going to see very commonly is also a power struggle. Wherever there is normal love, which means any of those circumstances—repeating situations from our parents, their conflicts, their circumstances, repeating the protocol love of what we were taught from Hollywood, from the movies, from storybooks of what love is supposed to be—there is always going to be a power struggle. What the silver screen teaches us about love is just as dysfunctional and neurotic as what we got at home. It just looks better because it's got more glitz. These people have more cars, bigger houses, and maybe more jewelry and they are on private planes, but they are certainly neurotic; they're just more glamorous in their neuroses. Look at the rate of divorce, broken families, substance abuse, and so forth.[31] So again we have this discrepancy, this really diametrically

---

[30] Lawrence B. Schiamberg, *Human Development* (New York: Macmillan, 1985), 57-69; John Bradshaw, *Creating Love* (New York: Bantam, 1992), 9.

[31] Glenda Riley, *Divorce, An American Tradition* (New York: Oxford University Press, 1991), 171-173.

opposed life. Somewhere in us we say, "Life is good." That's what we say. This is what we desire in us.

What It Really Is

Here's where we're going to see the flip side of this in the natural love. If I asked you what is your desire in love, rather than what your experience in love is, you'd put down two different answers. If I asked, "What is your desire in love?" everybody would have a really wholesome, good idea. It's going to be filled with words like *respect, laughter, caring, sharing, strength, peace, kindness, reaching out to others*, and *service*, and it's experiencing God's creation together, through each other. That's what we would probably say. But on the flip side, I'd say, "So, tell me about your last couple of years in relationships." "Oh, God, how much time do you have? Just the last one alone . . ."

What is it that really dictates what we think is normal? We think romance doesn't last; we think the goodness doesn't last; we think the good feeling doesn't last. Yet our true identities and goals are to do what? To feel good about ourselves and to feel good with others in a mutual respect, to share, to be happy. Nobody gets up in the morning and says, "Yup, I'm in love. I think I'm going to be as rotten and nasty as I can be." But yet, we function in those direct opposites. We have this normal love, which comes from what we're taught, which also comes from what we're taught in the home. Then we grow up, we're in our teens, we're in our twenties, and we have our idea of love, which causes another problem because we say to ourselves, "The kind of love I want I guess I'll never get." Again, these examples of normal love, to me, spell nothing but hopelessness and helplessness once you give your heart away. To me, the idea of giving your heart away means missing an organ. If I gave of myself 110 percent and I got nothing back, there's such a fear of "As soon as I give, I will be taken." These are all examples of the common normal love.

Listen to the radio. Listen to the songs on the radio. Some artists are mindful and enlightened and have a spiritual basis, but outside of that the common love song is the blues. It's about somebody who's stuck in a bar at three o'clock in the morning, stuck in a smoke-filled room where nobody can even breathe, and the patrons are swapping their stories of love. "She left me; he left me; took the money, took the kids." It's like that old joke about what you get when you play a country western song backwards: You get your house back, your horse back, your girlfriend back.

That's what's underneath this, and that's what we normally expect. In fact, we're very predictable when we meet people. This is not just about romantic love. This is about all love. All love is the same, as we're going to see when we get into relationships at work, with coworkers, employees, employers, bosses, and supervisors. If you're the manager, perhaps it's "Don't get too close." We're using that same normal something that says if you get in there and you trust and you give it your all, you're going to be taken advantage of, which again says that we normally believe closeness breeds an annihilation of self. "I'll lose myself in you." It's again breeding the power struggle. Somebody's dominant and somebody is submissive. We do it in families, we do it on the job, we do it with strangers. Not right away—when we first meet people, we appear equal, only because we are showing our best side, whatever that means. And when you show your best side, you're implying that you have a bad side. Opposites are also equally true, so if you put your best foot forward, it implies the other one is lame. Again, a conflict. We live and breathe conflicts and contradictions, especially when we get to this *love* word. We are sure that love hurts. If love feels good for too long, it scares us. It's going too well. Something's going to happen. Laugh today; cry tomorrow. Again, this is what we are taught normally.

So what usually happens? Where does this natural love come from? Is there a natural love that we have been taught? Subtly, faintly, vaguely, we have been taught about natural love. You have an idea about natural love when you start to think about how you want your *desire self*, how you really want love to be. When you get to that, you are getting to the real you. You're getting to a more natural you rather than this taught and carved-out-of-experience you. So if you're looking for your definition of *love*, you've got to go into two pockets. The first pocket is your experience. What have you experienced in life with love? You will find that you have probably experienced trust and mistrust, betrayal, hurt, pain, taking advantage as well as being taken advantage of. If you're going to be honest, you'll see you've been on both sides, where you have dominated and where you also have been dominated, all through your life, and do not limit this analysis or inventory to just romantic love. Think of your relationships with your brothers, your sisters, your mother, your father, your children, aunts, uncles, cousins, friends, coworkers, as well as spouses and people with whom you've been intimate, because you're going to see that there is a pattern and the pattern is it's a dominant-submissive kind of power struggle that suddenly ripples through all of it. No matter how hard you try as you get up in the morning to say, "Today is the day that I will experience love differently," something seems to happen that sabotages it.

We also have people who stay frozen, who have experienced normal love, who have a desire self that says, "This is really what I believe love is." (We haven't defined it yet, but it will be a definition to help you break these confines of normalcy and break into what is truly and naturally you. You can then write your own script rather than simply imitating a script that you were handed.) We have people who have gone through all that, and they literally put the brakes on their emotional lives. They just stop. "I will not let myself feel." Why? Because they have experienced that whenever they felt something, they lost themselves, and the only way to hold on—to their identities, their power, being in charge, being in control, being the master of their own ships—is to not let any feelings out, and so what these people do is they remain noncommunicative about matters of the heart. They live very cerebral lives. They could be highly intelligent, talk about a whole lot of stuff, but heart to heart they will not touch the subject. If they do, briefly, it's just that—briefly.

Now, what happens to a person like that? It mounts and builds, but because it is normal and not natural, they crack. Something will happen. Life is an orderly existence. It exudes order. And life is really about a lesson in loving more and more every day, not less and less. Any more than we can stop the sun from rising and the sun from setting, you cannot stop your natural need and desire to love and to be loved. It is what you get up in the morning for. It is why you are alive: to learn that expression of who you are, to love and be loved. Life will win, meaning the higher order of things, the Author of Life, which is the Author of Love—they're the same—wins.

What does that mean? Sooner or later you will come to an understanding, even if it's on your death's door, that there is no greater way to live life than to love and be loved, as often and as deeply as you can. The problem is not the desire to live that way, but to know how to live that way. As long as we're stuck in a normal pocket of love, we will leave the planet brokenhearted; we'll have had glimpses of it, phases of it, and more pain, I believe, than what is really necessary. I have seen many relationships die simply because of the wrong definition. There was enough love between the people, but they couldn't get out. They couldn't get out of the trap of the confines of what they had normally experienced, habitually and behaviorally experienced, year after year in life. They were habitually addicted to "This is the way I am, I can't change, this is all I know," and they stayed that way. So if people come from a controlling family, they stay controlling their family, never seeing three sides of the story, which is yours, theirs, and the truth. There are always three sides.

If you came from a family of screamers, you never learned how to speak calmly. Maybe you came from a family that said criticism builds strength, which happened in people who were born during the war, during the depression, during which they couldn't address the pain because it was so raw. They were on a battlefield, in some cases literally, in their own childhoods, and they were taught, "Don't cry." They were taught, "Don't talk about the heart, don't talk about feelings—we've got to be strong for each other." So now, they get married and they have their kids, and they believe they're building strength in their children by nitpicking: "Oh, you got a B+? How come you didn't get an A?" It's never good enough; that's the syndrome. Whatever you do, it's never good enough. So what do you do? You go out and find somebody—a boss or a spouse—who picks at you and nags you and reminds you of the same things you came from, and in the meantime your heart is so full with the desire to just have somebody see you in some healthy and positive and important way, and you can't get out. Meanwhile, that person who's nitpicking at you may in his or her heart deeply love you, but can't get out of the mold that says, "Don't express anything positive to another person, because that's not what we're taught." We repeat this over and over, from generation to generation, and this is what happens normally in love. This is not natural. Let's look at what natural love is.

Natural love comes from nature. If it comes from nature, it comes from the same author as the one who created nature. What is natural about you is your ability to love the same way the one who created you loves. You are a part of nature. You are truly made of the same substance as nature, the same molecular structure; atomic and subatomic particles that make up a star that glistens and shines across the black night are the same things that we are made of.[32] That is exciting and powerful natural news about you. There have been scientific discoveries about how all of nature connects and interconnects.[33] Biochemist Cleve Baxter has done numerous experiments registering the increase of energy when people walk

---

[32] Carl Sagan, *Broca's Brain* (New York: Random House, 1974), 15-18.

[33] Sagan, *Broca's Brain*, 15-18.

into the room.[34] This is similar to plants responding to owners. The plant says, "Ooh, maybe I'm going to get water now. Ooh, maybe they'll turn me around. I can get sun on the back of that little fern there." Now we're seeing this evidence, and we're getting closer and closer to what is natural about us. The same thread of light that moves through the stars and moves through the sunshine and moves through and makes and casts shadows from mountains and valleys and makes the ripples in the ocean and causes the foam as the tides pull in and out is the same power that we are breathing. That's nature. That is what's natural about you.

The same way I can divide normal love as experiential, I can now say natural love is what is inherited. You were born with this ability to imitate what you have been given by your Creator. It is your inheritance. Your breathing is an inheritance. This connection with all life is an inheritance. In the same way that we might have inherited some of these normalcies, the big shift in one's love life is the ability to get out of what may have been normal for you, simply because it was a habit, and move into what is natural to you because you have inherited it and learn about that capacity. Usually, when people talk about love and how they grow in love, they're in a normal love relationship at first. There's a conflict and then they resolve it. If there's enough love and enough real spiritual connection, they grow out of it and heal.

My approach here is to start not from pathology, but rather to start from your true, divine self. The normal love follows the human self, the finite, limited self, but the natural love comes from your true self, your divine self, and I want to begin to talk about love and our relationships in love with people and the whole world, our whole global perspective, from talking about what is natural to you because it is not something you have to go and get. You have enough love in

---

[34]   Robert Stone, Ph.D., *The Secret Life of Your Cells* (West Chester, PA: Whitford Press, 1989), 30-32.

you right now to literally change the course of life as we know it in this twenty-first century and forever. You do not have to go and get more love any more than you have to go to a special breathing tank to get more air. It is the quality of how you breathe—that is, if you took time to THINK as you're breathing, your body would change, the cells of your body would change, rather than just breathing. "Well, that's all I've got time for—a quick gulp. That's all I've got time for. Oops! I'm sorry, toes, not today. You're not going to get fed." Realize this gift—that you are breathing—who are you without it, by the way?

That is your inheritance, and so now this natural definition of *love* is for me the full expression of life's goodness. This is my definition of *love*, the natural kind. It's a definition. It is the full capacity of life's expression, expressing through everything you do, say, think, and feel. When I use the word *life*, I also can use it interchangeably with the word *power*, with the word *love*, with the word *God*, because for me they are all the same. What is natural about you is that you are already powerful. What makes you powerful is not your position, not your degrees, not your home, not how good your hair came out today. What makes you powerful is that what you are breathing inside of you is the full power of God. It already exists in you, so right from there is the biggest conflict with this normal definition of *love*, which tells us go out and get it, while this natural definition of *love* says that you already have it. It also doesn't say, "You're nobody till somebody loves you," which is what normally is said. What is said here is, "You are somebody wonderful because God loves you and created you with the full power of love within you."

So what is natural about you is that you already are loved, have love, breathe love, and the love from this natural side has within it the capacity for order and harmony, like we see in the universe. The rings around Saturn don't go into therapy to discuss the rate of speed that they're going to travel. It is innate to inner rings that there is a harmonious orbital factor among them that automatically matches the twelve moons around Jupiter and causes just enough gravitational pull in all directions so the solar system stays in harmony. That is a loving solar system. That is a community of energies, and the way that it was designed and the way that it is created is that it is innately within it to stay in harmony. That's what it does. It doesn't have to go get harmony. Mars and Mercury do not have to meet at their planetary weekly meeting to learn about how to get harmonious; it's in them already. It is in us already to be in love, in harmony with each other, with life, in accord with the laws of life, because we are a part of nature.

Then why do we have problems and so much conflict and so much pain in love? The conflict is that we are coming out of this normal love construct rather than a natural love construct. The natural love says, "You are good, for goodness sake." That's what it starts with. It says that no matter who your mother and your father were, no matter what dynamics came out of your family—we all have something, and that something was to jump start us, I believe—you have to go deeper inside of yourself to find what is natural about you, rather than to follow like a dog chasing a bone what is normal out in the world.

For me, I believe we all, in some fashion or another, come from dysfunctional families, and I believe that your family and my family are perfectly imperfect. Perfectly imperfect. Why? Because it's not their job to be perfect to you, for you, for your sake. There's only one source that can be perfect, and that's inside of you. If we were to adhere to our parents as perfect expressions of man and woman, we would be worshipping them as false idols. It would be paganistic, and so when we simply come to an understanding that our mothers and fathers and families are people in the world, and when you make a shift in your mind that says your father was a man first, your mother was a woman first, in terms of roles, and they only functioned in the mother-father role for a short time, then you will free them up and free yourself up, because the longer you hold them in the role of mother and father, the longer you trap yourself in the role of son or daughter, and that is not the only role, the only hat you will ever wear. You are a person first, then you are incidentally male or female, and then you may be incidentally a parent yourself, or a spouse yourself, but you are a person first, and the source of your life is and always will be the one who gave you life in the first place—not biological life, but all life for all time—and that is your Creator.

And so there is a huge breakthrough that happens when we let go of our family as being responsible for shaping and molding and sculpting us into who we are. We will break out of that normal pocket of what love is and open into a wide open field, free about what natural love is. You will also go back and love the very people who may have hurt you because, in fact, you will understand they didn't hurt you. What did they do? They poked you to do what? To go find the source, find the power. This is the first time on the planet that there are hundreds and hundreds and hundreds of books, tapes, videos, seminars on the shelves that say, "Go within and free thyself." We are the first generation that has been handed that torch, and what I say we have to do is take it and stand up so that the children of the world will see it. Be the example of it. Get them off the hook. You'll get yourself off the other hook. Then you'll stop running into your mother and your father with every boss you meet, with every friend you meet, with every relationship, with every friend, with every time you get married, every time you get divorced, every time you get re-married, every time you get divorced again.

What is natural about you is your ability to love. Is love a feeling or a thought? Love to me is the thought of God in me and the awareness that the same power that is God is through my breath and through my veins and through my bones and through my muscles and through my cells, and I will feel that as power and I will feel joy. Is love a thought? Yes, it is the thought of God. It is the thought of God in every breath you take that is a promise, a signature upon your soul that says you are safe no matter what. From Isaiah in the Old Testament, "Behold I am with you in all days, even to the ends of the earth" (Isa. 41:8-13). He says, "Be still and know that I am God" (Isa. 41:13-14), which means stop your chatter, stop the analyzing in your head. Be still. Go inside your house, in your heart, and just feel it. What will you feel? Probably your own tension first, and the longer you sit it will peel off, and for however long it takes that just means you've got to peel off another layer; so if it takes a thousand hours, it means you had a thousand layers, but the bottom of this is endless in our capacity to love and to be loved. This is what is natural.

For me to talk about relationships, about your true power and your true essence, I have to start with how you are created, and that is not pathological. **Your pathology is only a temporary overlay.**[35] And it spurs on your search to go within and free up. All of your life is a love story. Every person you meet will help you to love yourself more. What is natural about love is that it is good, it is peaceful, and it always brings the best out in you. If it brings out the worst, it's not natural—it's neurotic. There's a mouthful. Natural love always brings out the best in you, so what do we do with the expression, "We always hurt the one we love"? Get rid of it. Love is not a license to do what you want with another human being on any level. Love brings out the best in you, and the best part about you is power, is God, is wisdom, is God, is kindness, is God, is strength, is God, is peace, is God, is healing—it's God. All those words are just adjectives for the Creator. This is who you are at your best.

Your whole trip on earth is to experience becoming God-like. Well, there's another catchy saying. So what does "Made in the image and likeness" mean? Here's what I believe. To me, made in the image means I am shaped just like—like a reflection, like a mirror's reflection. I am shaped just like—image, small version of. Is it in my body? No, God would never have picked these thighs. Trust me. So where is it? It is inside of me; it is in the spirit of me; it is in

---

[35] Foundation for Inner Peace, *A Course in Miracles* (Farmingdale, NY: Coleman Graphics, 1975), 2:110.

the light that I am, which is the image of God. My very flesh right now is pouring through and radiating with God's sunshine—this is who I am. In fact, if you want to know what you really look like, you look like you swallowed sunshine and it's poking out of every pore of your body, and no matter where you walk there's literally radiant sunshine that is making a 360-degree trail in front of you, behind you, around you, and wherever you go you're leaving a trail of light and love. That's when you become conscious of natural love. If you're stuck in normal love, you're probably moaning about something that somebody didn't do or could have done, how come he/she didn't call, what could have been, "Why didn't . . . ?" and "I'm always the one. Well, I'm not bringing it up this time." That's the normal love. The normal love is get as much as you can—and, by the way, what are we going to do with it, since we're all going to go to the same place anyway? I hear getting through the portal from this dimension to the next dimension has a very brief express line where you are only able to enter with one item or less, and that item is your attitude, not your materialistic baggage.

So what I really look like is sunshine and I'm wearing a body. In fact, the body will change its cells every eleven to twelve months, says Deepak Chopra,[36] but the light within stays, and it is the attitude and my interaction with that light that actually creates the atmosphere in the body called *health* or *disease*. My first love affair, my primary love cause, must be with my power source, or I will go out in the world and think I'm an empty, clanging shell, and I'll go and look for people who look like they have light and try desperately to hold onto it, because they look like they've got light. That's why we like to go after somebody with whom we will identify as having some power. The chemistry that we speak about is usually somebody who exudes power or confidence, and it's usually false. It's usually just in

---

[36]   Chopra, *Ageless Body*, 114-118.

some gear—some made-up something. It's their style: "I love the way you walk."

You have power in you right now to do absolutely anything you want, beginning with your own life, your own body, your own family, your own anything. The power that made the body can heal the body. This is how you've been designed; it is natural. The best of you is brought out when you identify all that you do from a natural love cause. The minute you're off your mark, the minute you're off center, know that you slipped over into the normal pocket and the normal pocket of love is hopeless, helpless, despairing, and in conflict, with victims and rescuers and betrayals, and what is natural about love is that all layers of you commingle in a harmonious way simply to get better and better and better. All layers of you include physically, emotionally, financially, mentally, and spiritually. And I must be able to first recognize this in myself before I could ever be in exchange of it with someone else.

Continuing in this same conflict of normal love versus natural love, we have then a conflict in the description itself. The normal love will always shape us into a *blame-shame me*, because it encourages conflict and it encourages lack—"I'm not enough; I'm not good enough"—because of the rescue-victim roles that will get played out. And so the underlying thing there is that the self, who you are, is not enough; that "not enough" says you're lacking something. There's something that's not okay about you. A lot of industries make a lot of money out of the fact that they can further encourage and reinforce that we are not enough, and so we can put lots of money into externals (cosmetics, fashion, attitudes, body shaping-reshaping, etc.) because we have to have a certain look, a certain flair, a certain style, to try to make up for what we feel we don't have enough of.

The end result is that we will think of ourselves in a subtle and subconscious way as harboring a shame, a *shame-blame*. If I'm ashamed of something, I'm usually going to blame somebody. What this does in the shame-me, blame-me is it will absolutely keep a wall, a defense, between myself and whomever it is that I want to love or want to love me. This normal pocket definition of *love* is again based on finites and lacks and deprivations, and I have to go and get more to be more. So when I get close to someone, I can only get so close, because I'm convinced if I let them in all the way, they will see that I'm really not enough. I'm not good enough, smart enough, tall enough, short enough, rich enough, sexy enough, passionate enough; I don't cook; I don't clean; I don't iron right—all the things that we somehow feel are important to get people to care about us and stay with us. So I put up a wall because I'm sure of this "I'm not enough" tag in me. I'm sure. I've been convinced by life's experiences that the love I attract doesn't last; the love I attract is painful; the love I attract is wrapped around substance; the love I attract has to do with victims and rescuers and power struggles and obsessions and possessions, securities and insecurities. And so I'm convinced then by experience that it must be because I'm the defective model. I'm also convinced that other people have a whole lot more love in their lives than I do. "So and so, you know, they've been going around together for years." (That's because they met in a revolving door.)

So now I am convinced that I'm defective, which means I have something to hide—so I put up a wall. The closer I get to somebody, the closer somebody tries to get to me, the thicker I build the wall. I make excuses for the wall. What are the walls? The walls are something that I will announce by word or action that puts a condition on the way that I am to express myself to somebody or the other person is to express him/herself to me. I'll put a condition on it, such as, "Why do you have to do that that way? Don't you know it annoys me when you do that? How could you? Why are you doing that? This is the way I like it. If you loved me, you would do it this way. You know how I am." All those conditions are really flags—big, red, blaring flags that say the defense is up. It usually works both ways, by the way. This is never one-sided; this is always two-sided. So now we have two fences in the middle of the neighborhood called

"Love Thy Neighbor." The red flag about the defense is "Come close to me, love me, but don't know anything about me. Don't dare come on the other side of the wall because I am convinced you are going to find the part of me that I have announced to myself and convinced myself is not enough and I'm hiding." It's the shame me. I'm a defective model, and some people will also throw this off and say, "I'm a defective model because of my parents," that whole thing again, or "because of where I came from." After eighteen, give it up. After eighteen years old, stop complaining about where you came from. I can't in my right mind (or left mind) agree that you are stuck in a circumstance and still look at the natural model of who you are, which is that you have inherited the full power of God. I'm not taking away from anybody's experience in childhood. What I'm saying is you have been given the full capacity to overcome it, but what you have to do is shift the emphasis and look inside for sources, for the one source, rather than outside to a person, place, or thing to make up for whatever it is that you didn't get. You will then go back to making false idols out of your parents, either for positive or negative reasons. There's the positive false idol of a parent where the parents have so taken care of, overprotected, and spoiled the kids that the kids can't go out on their own anymore because they're convinced that the world is not going to treat them like that, and they're right, and that's exactly why they've got to cut the string and go out there.

Thus the results blame-me, shame-me: I'm ashamed of something. I'm ashamed of some inadequacy that I have assigned myself to. The red flare about it is when one party—and it's usually both—puts conditions on the way that you're going to relate and communicate with each other. And this doesn't matter whether you are brothers, sisters, mothers, fathers, sons, daughters, siblings, spouses, husbands and wives, business partners, employees or employers—the name of the game is the same. When you put a condition on the person, you are saying to the person, "You are not okay the way you are." What you're saying is, "I love you if you totally change your DNA structure and become something else that I feel is more suitable to me." You have totally invalidated the other person.

Now, you'll usually find somebody who attacks and somebody who always feels that he or she is getting attacked. That's the match made in normalcy heaven. Somebody pokes the finger and criticizes, and somebody takes the blame. That's a match made in heaven—the normalcy heaven—but it's not natural heaven. And the victim says, "Well, I know what he means and that's the way he is; he's not going to change" or "I know how she is and she's not going to change," and that is enabling, because what that's saying is, "You're not okay the way you are" on both parts.

Love is the expression of the fullness that is God in you in everything that you say and do and think and feel. The very essence of God is with no conditions. So when I start putting conditions on somebody—including myself, by the way—I am not loving myself. Here's our first culprit. What conditions do you have on yourself? I can't, I won't, I'm too old, I'm too short, I'm too tall, I have a crooked pinky. What will people say? Whatever limits, a limit is a condition you have put on yourself, meaning whatever opinion you have of yourself, which is, "Well, this is just the way I am. You know, I flare up and then I get over it and deal with it. Well, I procrastinate and then deal with it. You know, and I'm a slob, and if I've got one blue sock on and one green—well, I'll deal with it." Any of those limits you put onto yourself is coming from the shame-blame me. You feel inadequate because you have not yet gone deep enough into yourself to find out what the God within you feels like. Most of the time we are taught about God from a cerebral package. We are taught about spiritual values, and we're taught about God from some kind of rulebook: a taskmaster, a big CEO in the sky, a controlling, father-type parent who says, "Do this or else," a reward-and-punishment God. And that is not the essence at all. In fact, the only way I believe you come to learn how God is, is to let God teach you and not to accept it from a book or somebody else's interpretation, and the only way you're going to give God a chance and therefore give yourself a chance to love yourself is by sitting in silence on a regular basis, and in the silence what is not you will simply bubble up to the surface and peel off. The oldest form of meditation is silence, and in the silence what you're going to be left with is the true essence of who you are, and you will come to know your goodness.

That brings us to the other side, to the natural definition of *love*. The real you is the *goodness you*. You are filled with goodness—always have been and always will be. The real you is the goodness you, the valuable you. You are valuable not because of your deeds in the world, not because of any plaques on the wall, not because of how many acknowledgments you have received, not because of any grading system. You are good because the Author who created you is good. The apple doesn't fall far from the tree. You are of the same source, the same substance. Just as we started in the definition that the image is the light within me, the second part of that image and likeness is the word *likeness*. The more that I act out in the world from this goodness me, the more I am acting as if God is acting. So the likeness part comes from acknowledging the goodness place within me and then thinking and doing and feeling out of that goodness place. You are good for goodness' sake and that was given—not earned or learned, but given. That's the power. It works toward the good of all. That's the innate intelligence in you that seeks always order and harmony.

Look at the condition of the world. The condition of the world is absolutely out of focus because people believe that they're not good, that they are defective models. They believe somebody else can take their power and so they fight, they war. They believe somebody else is more powerful, so they try to store in their barns in some financial or economic sense, as if that will then give them some credence to goodness, and it can't. They draw a small circumference around their lives and call it a comfort zone, because they think, *This is the only place I can be me*, because they fear public opinion for one reason or another, not knowing that anybody's opinion, including one's own, doesn't count because it is just as limited as somebody else's. We can't even keep track of how many times people have said whatever they've said about us, and it has no power. The one that is crippling your goodness is your own opinion of yourself, and that is the constant battle that we go through, the shame me versus the *goodness me*. The shame me is in the normal definition of *love* and the goodness me is in the natural definition of *love*, and there's the conflict. Remember, if you say somebody brings out the best in you, you're implying that the other side is the worst, and so we make these strong divisions in ourselves, the good you and the bad you, and that is not the truth. What you have is simply your opinion of yourself in contradiction and conflict with the truth about yourself. We're fighting the truth. As much as we go out there to seek power and love, it's as much effort as we put, I believe, to stop it, because we are afraid. If I am naked in front of you, you will see my imperfections. Your imperfections are there, because we are all on the road to becoming sunshine kids, and this never takes away from our value. **Your value is permanent**. You recognizing your value is what is called growth. Your value is innate and you are permanently good.

The usual question here is, What about the murderer, the rapist, the thief, and the psychopathic killer? What about them? Simple. They're just more steeped in the conviction that they're worthless, that they're useless, that evil triumphs, and they want to be on the winning team, so they do what typically was done to them. They are totally devoid of any true understanding of who God is or what that source of life is about. They are split in themselves, and they've lost the way back.

Affirmation, meditation, prayer is the way back home to the natural self, and finally, for the first time, it is acceptable. All the books on the shelves are saying the same thing: Go within. We went so far outside of ourselves to persons, places, and things, to fame, to fortune, and to power, and we came home empty, not feeling any better about ourselves. Finally, there's enough scientific data that shows that when you love, your cells change. That is exciting. It says that I don't need to love you. I desire to give my love to you, and by law what I send out comes back. That is the law of cause and effect, which is as certain as gravity.

But what happens to us in relationships is again this conflict—this double exposure, psychological cataract, which is an overlay on our perception of truth. We go out into the world seeking love and to be loved without ever learning how to love the self. How can I get or give what I don't think I already have? If I go out empty of love, by law I'm going to go find somebody who is just as empty, because what I send out is what comes back, and so what we have, which has been called the *codependency rage* over the last couple of decades, is really a lot of insecure people hooking up together, trying to make a whole person.

I can remember that a long, long time ago I used to call it my *Swiss cheese theory*, and I felt that a lot of people looked at relationships as if there were two pieces of Swiss cheese. Each piece has a bunch of holes in it. You slap them together and some of the holes get covered, and they figure some of that is better than being a whole piece of cheese, because you never think you're ever going to get to be a whole piece of cheese by yourself. So what you get is a codependent addiction to another person because you say, "I can't live if living is without you."

Most of the songs, again, what are they about? They're more about betrayal and hurt and pain. Look at the greatest love story in the world. Please, not the one with Ali McGraw in it! Not that one, but the greatest love story in history, in literature: *Romeo and Juliet*. They both died. Is that not a perfect example of that childhood story? They were so in love they killed each other because nobody would let them be together. I mean, where is, "They laughed, they grew old, they got gray hair, his teeth and his hair fell out," and you know, "They got a little chubby but they dance so 'cute' together. They both waddle the same now, you know"? Whatever happened to that? Where did that go? And that's what we all want, isn't it? We want to grow old together. Well, not with that model of love, we're not. We'll kill each other first.

So, when we get to be with people, we take the shame self and we hide it. This is again assuming that there is a shame self to hide. And then we look blaringly at the other person with this mask on and when he gets close, we give him conditions. We give him conditions like, "Did you have to fold the towels like that? I fold them in threes. Why did you fold them in half?" "You know that I like the sheets ironed. These haven't been ironed. This is just shy of sleeping with the enemy." As soon as we start putting these conditions, the big, red flag appears: "I'm afraid you're gonna find out that I'm a shameful kid," which means what? In my experiential normal definition of love, I was told what? "Bad, bad. Bad boy. Bad girl. Go to your room."

I don't care how many books you read to understand love; I don't care how many stargazers you go to; I don't care if you go to Madam Babushka on the boardwalk who says she's a medium (but when you get close up, she's really an extra large). I don't care where you go to find out what you think love is, I will tell you you need to go inside yourself and come to know God. The nature of love is not human at all. Walking, talking, working, counting change, flipping a hamburger, throwing pizza dough in the air is human, but love is divine. It is God's very life in yours.

The true essence of love is God in your life. If you want love, if you want to feel real love, then be still and be quiet, and in the silence let the Author of Love directly teach you about love. You will not learn about love from another person. You will see it exemplified, but you cannot learn about love except from its Author, and that is God. We reflect it, but the fullness of it can only come when you allow yourself to give over your opinions and definitions of yourself, of your life, of your needs, and listen to the still point in the center of the wheel, as William Johnston calls it in the book called *Silent Music*, and know that that spot when you end a breath and begin to take the next is where God waits for you. Every day God waits for you. Every breath you take is a constant whisper: "I love you no matter what. I love you no matter what. I love you no matter what." Only in silence can we bring all the misery, all the heartaches, all the burdens, all the shame, all the blame into that private prayer place inside. Even if you don't believe in God, guess what? That doesn't count. Take your disbelief in with you. Take your anger toward the power with you. And then say, "Teach me the truth about love."

Your Worksheet A

I want to do an exercise now to help us begin the process to learn what the real feeling of love is like so we will recognize it in ourselves and in each other, so that we can then continue to really live in loving relationships.

- Make yourself comfortable. Sit in a comfortable position in the chair. Again, if you'd like to, take your glasses off. Feet on the floor, leave your hands loose on your lap, unfold your arms, and close your eyes.
- Take a deep breath and go deeper with each breath, and take another deep breath. Begin to quiet yourself by simply repeating the word *relax*, and by repeating the affirmation several times, silently to yourself, ten times or more:

  I can relax, for I am good. I can relax, for I am good. I can relax, for within me there is good, for goodness' sake.

  And continue to relax, breathing in and breathing out. Relax and go deeper.
- Create a beautiful picture for yourself, one that will represent all elements of nature, living and breathing and cohabiting in harmony. So in your own way you create a garden of love, a garden of happiness, your own version of the garden of

goodness, of paradise, where you see all life, including trees and vegetation and mountains and valleys and streams, and animals of all kinds, and sun and sky and stars and day and night, knowing that where you live is a part of a bigger place called the solar system, called the galaxy, called the universe, and where you are is a place in the universe that you call life, just where you're living right here and right now. Make the picture as peaceful and happy as you can, sensing all kinds of people, from children to the aged—all races, all creeds, all kinds of people, simply present and even singing and dancing, just cohabiting and living, and right where you are, right here and right now, you begin simply to feel the peace of a harmonious nature that surrounds you, a gentleness in the way the sky outlines mountains and the sun casts its shadow, moving through the trees' leaves. Notice how many colors can be captured in one butterfly, how many sounds can be sung from one bird, and you, the highest creature in this garden, you, the highest level of creation on this planet, live and breathe and think and make choices. This is the power of God moving through you. You now make the choice fully to feel your goodness, for goodness' sake, and to feel your value because of who created you. Not by your own deeds, but because of the one who breathes when you breathe. Then in silence, simply ask: "Teach me the truth about love. Teach me the truth about me in love." Then in silence be still and listen and trust the first feeling or impression or response.

• Take as much time as you need. When you are comfortable to do so, just open your eyes and begin to make your own notations, your own responses to these feelings and impressions from deep inside.

It is recommended to do this every day, even to keep a record, a journal of these impressions, and in this you will know the teacher of love and life is within you. In this all shame dissolves and you will be set free of all false images, opinions, and limitations that you might have placed upon yourself or that you have accepted from others. The more that you do this, the closer you get to your true you; for goodness' sake accept your goodness.[37]

---

[37] From the Foundation for Inner Peace, *A Course in Miracles*, Vol. II, Lesson 95 (Farmingdale, NY: Coleman Graphics, 1975), 164:

I am one self, united with my Creator.

You are one within yourself and one with Him. Yours is the unity of all creation. Your perfect unity makes change in you impossible. You do not accept this and you fail to realize it must be so only because you believe that you have changed yourself already. You see yourself as a ridiculous parody on God's creation—weak, vicious, ugly and sinful, miserable and beset with pain. Such is your version of yourself, a self divided into many roaring parts, separate from God and tenaciously held together by its erratic and capricious maker to which you pray.

Also, the prayer to Lesson 95: "I am one self, united with my Creator, at one with every aspect of creation and limitless in power and in peace."

The following excerpts are valuable as well. The first is from Mihaly Csikszentmihalyi, *The Evolving Self, A Psychology for the Third Millennium* (New York: Harper Collins, 1993), 22:

The picture of the self we usually have is that of a homunculus, a tiny person sitting somewhere inside the brain who monitors what comes through the eyes and ears and other senses and evaluates this information, then pulls some levers that make us act in certain ways. We think of this miniature being as someone very sensitive and intelligent, the master of the machinery of the body.

Your Worksheet B

The first remedy healing exercise that we're going to do is to get us through a visualization to peel away what is normal about us in love and to let stand what is natural about us in love. All you need to do is be comfortable and close your eyes.

Those who conceive of it as the soul believe that it is the breath of God that transformed our common clay into a mortal envelope for the divine spark.

And finally, from Sondra Ray, *Loving Relationships* (Berkeley, CA: Celestial Arts, 1980), 4:

If you want your personal relationships to work, you must get clear on your relationship to God. When you are clear about who or what God is, then you have all the help you need for your relationships. If you are not clear about God, you may try to blame God for your troubles or even think that God punishes you or is out to get you. God is the source from which everything and everyone comes. If you don't have a relationship with the source, how can you have a good relationship with people? How can you love someone when you don't love the source? To have a good relationship with God, you must have some idea about God and God has always been a difficult concept for people to understand. You may have felt confused about this and you may have also felt guilty as you searched for the truth, especially if you've had a strong childhood background in an orthodox religion. It may seem disloyal to your parents and religious leaders to consider breaking away from the creed that you were taught as a child. However, such a search does not have to be destructive. It can enlarge upon your childhood conceptions and may strengthen them.

- Allow yourself now to just be in a comfortable position. Your feet are fine and flat on the floor; just let your hands be comfortable on your lap. If you wear glasses, you might want to take them off. Let your hands be loose and comfortable in your lap, and the only thing that you need to do to begin this exercise is to pay close attention to your breathing. So keep your eyes closed and you'll simply continue to breathe in and to breathe out, in an easy and steady pace.

- Let each breath get a little deeper and a little slower, a little deeper and a little slower, and as you continue to do this, create that image of sunshine. Imagine that the sunshine is inside. Become childlike, playful, and imagine you literally drank from a cup of sunshine. Picture it, a gentle, soothing sunshine light that moves into every cell of your body. Even picture now that the rays of sunshine extend through the pores of your skin and radiate in a full 360-degree arena around you, and slowly to yourself you will repeat, "I am made of light from inside out." Just say it inside to yourself, silently.

> I am made of light from inside out. This light is good. This light is good. I am made of light from inside out. This light is love. This light is love. I am made of light from inside out. I am made of light from inside out. This light is God. This light is God, and in this I remain good for goodness' sake in all I do, say, think, and feel.

- Continue to just sense light and coordinate, associate that light is good, your light, you are good, from inside out.
- Relax and let a peaceful glow surround you and protect you, and know that the true you is a loving you for goodness' sake. Relax.

- It's good to repeat this as often as you can, in the morning when just awakening, even in the shower, as you're driving to work, as you're driving home from work, as you're entering into your home, as you are meeting others. The simple affirmation

  I am made of light. The light is good. The light is love. The light is God.

  shifts the consciousness of your true self into a more natural source, truly getting you to see you are love just because you've been created by the loving Creator, who left that loving signature, your breathing. When you are comfortable to do so, just open your eyes and keep the feeling of the goodness with you.

Chapter Seven

Living in Loving Relationships

What Happened to Me

The more I prayed, the more clearly I got to "see" myself. I began to see that all relationships were about lessons of love. Even if the relationships were painful, they still gave an opportunity for learning the truth about love.

A lesson comes to mind here that had occurred through a long-time friend. This friend was very smart, with a good sense of humor, and a person who had a "new problem" every week. If it wasn't her marriage, then it was an illness, the mortgage, the dryer, the boss, the neighbor, etc. We were friends from childhood. We certainly had shared lots of fun times. So, as adults we continued to stay in touch, dragging through all the "responsibilities." I thought one of these responsibilities was to always help her. After all, we were friends for so long. I thought I had to help "fix it," whatever it was. In time I became exhausted. My phone line became a "hotline." It cost me time, energy, and money!

Again, through my meditation, I reassessed myself. What are you doing? The lesson became clear: Loving friends don't "use" each other. This is perhaps best said by Melody Beattie in *Codependent No More*: "It [detachment] is not detaching from the person whom we care about, but from the agony of involvement."[38] I learned to "get out of the way" and let others find the "God within." Sometimes helping isn't helping at all.

How You See It

In order to talk about living in loving relationships, we should ask, What do these words mean? *Love* can have a normal connotation versus a denotation as being a natural love. In the same way, if we put together *living in loving relationships*, we have to come to some agreement about what are we talking about. I'm going to offer a window to look through, which I'm going to call a definition for that phrase; a starting point for us to get a little bit more in touch with why it is we can have a concept about love, and what happens when a function in love, which we call *relationships*, doesn't match the concept. What we're calling *love* is not what we are experiencing in the relationship.

There's a breakdown and *living in loving relationships* is a very short phrase, so there must be some discrepancy. There's a malfunction. Something happens to short-circuit our ideal of what we're calling *love* and the result, how we interact once we're with people, once we're interacting with them, and it doesn't even matter if it's a family member or a friend. It doesn't matter if it's coworkers. What I want to start with is just this idea of looking at the words *living, loving, relationships*, and see if we can try to uncover where this process malfunctions. From a definition of *love* into the function of relationship, we malfunction. We lose it. This is just a definition, a window to look through.

Now, I'm going to take them one at a time, so I will start with the word *living*. Words that I might use to describe it would be

---

[38] Melody Beattie, *Codependent No More* (New York: Harper and Row, 1987), 51.

breathing, growing, changing, healing in the now. It's living. It's alive now. If I look at the phrase *in loving*, then I'm going to make an equal sign to signify what might this mean. I would say it means the presence of love, because it's *in* love—that little preposition helping us to know that it's in it. So it's the presence of love. It's the act of loving. It's ongoing loving. It's response loving. It's communicating loving, because it's in loving. It is not a static condition when we give it action, loving. There's a dynamism to it, when I say *in loving* as opposed to just using the noun *love*.

Relationships. What would we say about relationships? I can have them with all types of people, all types, family, one on one. I can even have a relationship with myself. And a relationship with God. When I break the phrase *living in loving relationships* apart into those separate phrase words, I don't see a problem. We can come up with clear, accurate terms for *living*. We can come up with some clear, accurate terms for *in loving*, and clear, accurate terms for *relationships*.

What happens when I put it all together that makes us malfunction? I started out with a definition of *love*, and we broke it into two categories of normal love, which is wrapped in fear and predisposes to failures and feeling limited and finite, and brings a lot of what-ifs, and natural love, which is more alive and dynamic and says that the source of the power is on the inside, not on the outside. We're going to do the same thing for *living in loving relationships*.

Again, when I take the words apart, there isn't a problem. All of a sudden I put them together, and even if I asked, How can you be living in loving relationships? the malfunction occurs. Immediately you think of what usually happens to you. As soon as I get personal and speak to you, your idea shifts and gets out of the natural definition of *love* and falls into the pocket of normal love where the problems are. You might get uneasy as soon as I say, "So, how are your relationships? How is it living in loving relationships?" "Don't ask. Uh! Same old, same old—just a different day. Well, I try. I've tried everything." Again, there's really this kind of block or "It can only be so good."

Some of the attitudes that come up are things like "True love never runs smooth." Remember that? Why? "You always hurt the one you love." Look at this stuff that's underneath there. You see? "You have to be no good to be treated good?" What is that? Dear God! "Don't tell them everything. Even keep some secrets. This will make them wonder." Those are sixties', seventies' how-to stuff. That's what was going on then—you know, all the angles, the gimmicks. To get the right person, you've got to act like this and do like that. But it's not natural.

What it says is that you're not all right by yourself, that as soon as you start relating to another person you have to change the very fabric that you are. I have to change to catch him/her. I have to cast the fishing pole. I have to do the right thing. There are scores of case histories in therapists' offices about how the person whom someone married is not the same person that he or she is living with, even though it's only a few short years. People change right after the commitment. They get settled in and then it changes.

I would even question the need to work on a relationship, and I'll tell you why. Coming from the natural definition of *love*, it does not make sense to me to work on a relationship. I think it simply means that two people have to take full responsibility to work on themselves and the relationship will work itself out. If you have to work on a relationship, what you're really going to is a third party, like you're going to a lawyer—and I hope I'm not offending lawyers—to negotiate the best angle to convince the other party how he or she ought to change so that the two parties can become more compatible; somebody's got to compromise. I can't agree with that, because compromise says to me that I'm stifled or you're stifled. Where's the freedom to be? I know that God said I'm okay the way I am, and my only job and my only lesson is to be mindful of my fear, that if I am in fear I am not in love. If I'm in love with God and the source, I am not afraid, and that is the single thing that I am to pay attention to in my primary relationship, which is with God.

We sometimes do things backwards, especially in coupled relationships. The approach to me leaves something to be desired if it does not start out with: "You are responsible for your growth and I am responsible for my growth, equally." From that point, you either have two willing people who go side by side or you don't. You can't make anybody do anything, so my concept of relationship, again, is not how to make it work. I don't think you have to make it work. Why? Because to me, what is moving through the two of you is the presence of God. That's what you're in exchange about when you're relating to another person. You're literally seeing a reflection of God in this person that you did not see before, and in that reflection you are getting to know more about you.

A lot of what we call relationships in our culture is based on conditions of what we think the function of a relationship is. This is where the breakdown and the malfunction start. For the last century at least, except for this past decade, the main emphasis in relationship was security. It was the cornerstone of why people come together. People have learned to come together in relationships, and this is of all kinds, whether it's business, friendship, even family. We're going to do a little process to help bring this out. We come together; we pull together with each other for an underlying condition that we've been taught, which is security. You're nobody till somebody loves you. I'm not okay by myself. I need you to be fulfilled. I need you to remind me that I'm important. Now, right there, where's God? That is what I would say to my God, because to me that is the prayer, the surrender prayer, which I would say to my God: "I am nobody without you, Lord. You are the source of my content, my peace, and my joy. You are the source of my wisdom. You are the source for giving me value."

Again, the normal definition of *love* sets up this normal function for relationship which is security, and I believe that this continued throughout decades and decades as the effect of the industrial revolution, and what we did on an ongoing and regular basis, decade after decade, was to make machines, including computers, for everything. The reason for the industrial revolution was convenience for the human race, which is about the same thing that's happening for the computer age. It's for comfort and convenience. But what is happening as an effect of this industrial revolution is that we learned that the machine has more power than the "self."[39] We have placed the significance on the outside rather than the inside. The machine did it. The power is on the outside. We moved away from being an agricultural society. We moved away from connecting to the course of life in that creation. We moved away from the very vibration that we needed, and we mechanized ourselves right into being robot to robot in our relationships.

Now we're in a computer age. The same thing is happening, just at a different level, in a different octave. If we're not careful as we continue into the twenty-first century, we will fall prey. In the same way that we became machines as an effect of the industrial revolution, we will become isolated as a result of the computer age. Did you ever see a kid hour after hour on video games, or in front of a television, on XBox, or a person who just spends hours and hours at work at a PC and then comes home and does the same thing? They're relating to this two-dimensional screen. There's no life. The computer can do everything: it can talk; it can exchange; it gives you information, data. You feel a lot of power sitting in front of that computer. You put things in, you move that mouse around and make that little arrow thing go nuts. Now, it's got 4G wireless, it's got music, and graphics in 3D. It does everything but leap out and hug you. It will never do that. We're now becoming computers. From eighty years ago until

---

[39]   Robert A. Harper, *Psychoanalysis and Psychotherapy* (Englewood Cliffs, NJ: Prentice Hall, 1959), 171.

now we became machines, and the emphasis has been that the power is on the outside.

If I start with a normal definition of *love*, which is wrapped in a lot of conditions and fears and finites and what-ifs and where my childhood came from, etc., I am sitting prey to move into a relationship that's based on security. It says, "I need," whereas the natural definition says, "You don't have to go and get love; you already are loved." You are filled with the presence of love, and so the shift is when you're with someone, you're sharing the already given love with each other and seeing a new face of God in that other person. You don't need the other person, but you desire the exchange in order to learn more about how you can become more loving and more God-like. It's totally different in that you are not isolated, in that you are not the computer, just plugging in data back and forth to each other. You are getting closer to the source of you as it is reflected in another human being, including your children, spouses, coworkers, friends, and even strangers.

In fact, in the natural definition of *love*, there is no difference. There is no difference in what *A Course in Miracles*[40] would call a *special love relationship*. It says that we have special love relationships and *special hate relationships*, and that the reason why we set this up is based on what I'm calling the normal love definition, and therefore the normal relationship definition, which is security bound. What we do in a special love or hate relationship is we assign to people a script coming from the deficit, "I'm not enough by myself." It comes from "I need to be with you; I need to be in a relationship; I'm nobody till somebody loves me; all alone by the telephone; Saturday night is the loneliest night of the week." It starts when I give you a script. This is all subconscious. I meet you. There's some chemistry; there's some interaction—and I'm going to do this just with meeting of

---

[40]   Foundation for Inner Peace, *A Course in Miracles* (Farmingdale, NY: Coleman, 1975), 1:290.

people, then we're going to see how this applies to all relationships, even to children, spouses, coworkers, employees, employers, etc. But let's just say that you meet somebody and you have a chemistry. You start to do what I call the *me-too's*. The me-too's occur within the first week of meeting each other and in your conversation, no matter what the other person says, your response is "oh, me, too," because you desperately attempt to be connected to another human being. So what happens then is subconsciously we have handed a script to the person, and what we said to this person was, "I like you. I don't feel enough in myself. You will make me feel important. You will make me feel special. How are you going to do that? I'm going to tell you you're special and you're going to spit that back at me." That's what's called the special love relationship. This is all subconscious. We do this: "You're so special. I've never had this before. No one's ever looked at me quite that way before." What's he got? A third eye? I mean, do you know what I'm saying? It would be different if a Martian said it.

We hand this person a script. We do this subconsciously and it comes right out of us because we are following from the normal relationship definition, which is founded, grounded in security: "I need you. I'm not enough to function in my life. I have to be with somebody. I want to be with somebody, a partner. I have to, or I'll die." So, then what happens is again the chemistry, something clicks. It could be anything. "Oh, what's your sign?" You know, neon—whatever. I wanted my kids to have their names all lit up in lights, and I'm going to name them all Exit. (My jokes are always visual and they're never really good!)

I give this person the script subconsciously, and how do I do it? I feed him the very words that I want him to say to me. It's like you have an invisible signpost that says, "Okay, now, repeat after me: I think you're wonderful. I think you're the greatest thing since sliced bread"—and the Hallmark cards and the roses and the car, and ding dong, here it comes, "I'm going to bring you dinner," and all of it. I am not putting that down at all, but I think we absolutely need to celebrate everything. I personally believe every time you sit down to a meal with any human being who's still breathing, it is a celebration. There's a breath in that body, and when you sit down to break bread, to me that is a holy union, because when you are having a meal it is a very intimate thing—especially for an Italian like me. Even if you're breaking a cracker with another human being, you are going to ingest that, and what you are also going to ingest is the atmosphere in which you are talking, discussing, sharing. You are not just eating the food, you are consuming the energy, and the meal is a first and last time every time, because the energy is never the same, and I think that is a celebration.

I hate fast food. To me, there's nothing fast about eating. You have to understand where I come from. I was twenty-three years old and still asking to be excused from the table after about two hours, which at the time annoyed me, and now I don't even get up. The sun could come up and go down and we might still be sitting there, which is fine; you clean the tablecloth and start over. Here come the fruit and the nuts again, and I understand that as the absolute cornerstone for sharing and relating with people. Look at what has happened to families in the last two decades. Nobody sits down to eat together anymore—on the run, it's in the oven. It's like hospital food; you know, "nuke" it, rip off some Saran Wrap, and put it through your gullet. Now we have people who don't even eat anymore, they just shake and drink: "I don't have the time; just put it in a bottle, I'll shake it, gulp it." Be an astronaut if you want to do that. Of course, I am talking from my own experience, and you just have to throw out what you don't agree with and save the rest.

But I do think that the art of relating is just that: it's a special art that we have not learned because we have become so mechanized and isolated from each other. People come in and out from their houses—you know, back and forth to work—and what's the first thing they do when they come home? "Any mail? Dog go out? Water bill come? Pay the taxes?" We're so robotlike, and then you get people who are talking to each other while they're reading something—"Uh huh, uh huh, yeah, um hmm. No, I'm listening. Go ahead"—while they've got a phone stuck in their ear on the other side. This is what is normal about relationships, but to me it is not natural at all. It's not what I understand a relationship is.

You'll start to see where I'm going with the relationship—with a new definition, a natural relationship—when we start to break down those words of *living* and then *in loving* and *relationships*. Again, as we said, *living* means breathing, growing, changing, feeling, in the now; *in loving* means the presence of love, the act of loving, ongoing loving, response loving, communicating loving; and *relationship*, all types of people—family, one to one, having a relationship with yourself, and the primary relationship, which is with God.

What It Really Is

Let's go back to the special relationship. We handed the person the script and we said, "You be special to me because I don't feel special in myself." What you have done is you have set up exactly what the normal love is based on: a dominant and submissive pattern. You said, "You're up here, you're special, and I'm not, but when I'm with you I feel special," so the opposite is also equally true, which is that when I'm not with you, I'm going to do what? Panic. I'm going to fear. I'm going to have anxiety if you're not around. Why? Because I'm afraid that the one who validates me will not be around and then I'll have no value in this world. This is all subconscious. This is doomed. This setup is absolutely doomed. It is a time bomb. It is a walking, talking time bomb and it will explode. If I could predict six numbers like I can predict this, we all wouldn't have to worry. Sooner or later, in a short amount of time, what's going to happen is this special love interest is going to fall from the pedestal. Why? Because—big news bulletin—this person is not your God. The only one who is qualified to validate you is your Creator. Why? Because that's the only place your value comes from. It doesn't come from another person—not your mother or your father, not your brother or your sister, not your children, not your coworkers, not your spouses. No one makes you important. It is not what others are capable of doing. It's not their job, and yet this is the primary thing that we assign to people when we're with them in a relationship. "Well, after all, we're in a relationship." It's just such a clunky word—*relationship*. "Well, so, are you in a relationship?"

It will not take a whole lot of time before this special relationship person will make a mistake. Why? Because, well, this person is not walking on water; this person is human. He or she is going to say exactly the worst possible thing at the best possible time, and you're going to say, "I can't believe it. After all this time, how can you, in heaven and earth's name, say that to me? How could you have done that?" What you're really saying is, "Why did you not follow the script I originally gave you and why are you not my God?" That's what we do. And this person will make an error; it's just a matter of time—I'm talking a few short weeks. Think about yourself. How long do you go before you mess up in anything, and that includes procrastinating, getting angry at people, cutting people off—you know, giving people the international traffic signal out the window? How long does it take before we go a little off? What? A day, a week, an hour—isn't it going to happen? So, if you go off, what makes you think the other person's not going to do it? Well, the only thing that makes you think that is because you handed this person this special script that said, "Here, I want you to make me feel important, so read my lips. I'll tell you exactly what I want you to tell me. You just give it right back." And you're not saying this verbally; you're saying this subconsciously.

This is the exact same person who now turns into your special hate person, and you now make him or her the scapegoat for your life. "I can't believe it. You know, after all, it just changed; we were good together, we clicked." What is that, that clap on, clap off? What is that? "We clicked. We were like a dance. I never felt like that before." And we always have to throw this in: "The sex was great." Compared to what? Do you know what I mean? We always have to do this. Now what happened is that person didn't follow the script. That person now becomes the special hate relationship, and we now throw at that person everything that aggravates us.

Now I want you to know that you may have a hidden special hate relationship that is a little separate from you and not a member of the family, not somebody that you work with or for or who works for you. It may not be a spouse. It may not be a son or daughter. It may be—you ready?—the government, the Internal Revenue, the church, some institution—any group that you project that it's their fault you've made your special hate relationship. Wherever you have a special love relationship, you have a special hate relationship. It may not be exactly the same person. Sooner or later, though, the special love relationship will fall and become another special hate relationship, but you can have a separate, independent special hate relationship. It could be the medical society. It could be people with one green eye and one blue eye. It could be all tall people. Why do they have to do that? Just because they're tall? Doesn't that annoy you? You know, all short people. They just wiggle it; isn't it annoying? You see?

So our special hate relationships are directly related to our prejudices, and a prejudice is wrong. I don't care what you're prejudiced about, it's flat out wrong. It's just wrong. Preference is not prejudice. Preference does not say, "Because it's different, I judge it." So, it's different. I mean, even Baskin-Robbins has a variety. Your God is a God of variety. When are we going to get this? Did you ever see two birds the same? Two butterflies the same? Look at your garden and see how there isn't anything that's the same. There are not two snowflakes that are the same—not even two fingerprints that are the same. It is most ironic to me that there is such an abundance of variety in nature that we struggle all of our lives to go and be different and to be individual and to be unique, when that is something you never have to fight for. You already are that because you already are a one-of-a-kind, and the same thing we wanted ourselves, which is individuality, is what we are prejudiced against in other people just because they are who they are.

So we get trapped from a normal love definition in a normal relationship, which is absolutely going to set up special love and special hate interests, and again, it could be the government, authority, celebrities, people with a lot of money, poor people, people on welfare—anybody who doesn't fit our groove and who we can just, at will, throw a stone at. That is a special hate relationship, and bottom line, it's a judgment. Guess what? It's wrong. What it also means is that this is exactly what you're going to attract on a personal level for yourself, a judgmental relationship. Why? Because the law of the universe is simple, it is direct, it is clear, and it is independent of your opinion of it or your agreement with it. What I send out is what comes back. If I have a judgment out there, anywhere, it's because someplace I've judged myself and the world will judge me back, which is going to lead me to what I believe relationships are really about. There is no different kind of love. There's only one love. You don't love somebody differently. It's the function, the lesson, that is different, but love is love is love is love is love. The relationship simply means the form that the love is presently taking in order that the two individuals will learn more about themselves and draw closer to God and to their true image, their true nature.

So, what I would like to do is give a different name or a different definition for the function of relationship. The normal love gives the definition of *relationship* as "security"—it's out of need. In a natural love, relationship has a function, and the function is to help you to learn more about you, so you will come closer to the awareness of how God loves you. That is the function of any relationship. Now,

I'm going to use the same words again—*relationship* and *loving* and *living*—except that I'm going to identify them backwards. Instead of *living in loving relationships*, I'm going to now reverse the words to get another perspective on it.

What is really the definition of *relationship*? If I take the suffix off, which is the *ship* part, I see the word *relation*. What's the root word for the word *relation*? "To relate." What does that verb, *to relate*, really mean? It means "to retell." The suffix *ship* means "the condition," which means a form that we have chosen. To me, a relationship is a form in time and space in which two people have elected to retell their story, and that is why when you first meet somebody you spend so much time telling your story again. "When I was five, I was shorter than now, believe it or not." So the core essence of a relationship is that you are retelling the story of yourself to another person. Why? Because that person represents a new face of God's love back to you that's actually going to help you to retell the story of yourself now in a new and more empowered way, so that you will face the future not repeating the past.

Loving—what does really loving mean, simply, directly, and nonjudgmentally? It means that no matter what happens, you just don't judge it. Now, we are all judgmental. This does not have to do with how many novenas you said this week. We judge each other. You judge yourself. You're not good enough; you screwed up on this; how come? I should have loved more. The gravy didn't come out right. Whatever it is, you're judging, okay? The best way to tap in to how judgmental we really are is to choose a day in the week and have no opinion—regardless of what happens, stay very aware and have absolutely no opinion. Do you know how hard this is? For example, just deal with the weather. If it's too hot or too cold, we have an opinion about it. Like the weather's going to change: "Oh, I'm very sorry, we're going to drop the humidity right now." What good is the opinion? So watch how quick you are to be opinionated about absolutely everything. The toast is not right, whatever. It is totally an endless, endless account for how judgmental we can be. So if you want to get really clear and do a self-inventory, choose a day and start off with an hour. You will find that you don't have anything to say. Someone will say to you, "Oh, did you hear about so and so?" and if you're doing it right, if you're aware, you're not going to be able to respond because your immediate thing is, "Well, what I think—you know, and after all, what he really should be doing—I mean, come on now, is that the way to act? How could he do such a thing?" If there is anything that I have learned, it is that people will do absolutely anything. Do you understand that?

So the loving part, to me, means no judgment. *Good* is a judgment and so is *bad*. You know, people can flatter you and it's not for a good reason, because really what they're doing is setting you up for a special relationship. Do you know why it's not really important when people can say good things about you? It's because that is not adding even one iota of value to you, and if you think it does, then you have just put God on the unemployment line. That's his job. It's not your partner's job or your mother's job or your father's job to give you value. It's not your son's or your daughter's job to give you value. You don't have to get value; you've got value. But, you see, we don't know that, and so as soon as we get close to somebody, it's like we've held them captive. "Okay, you're going to give me value, right? Okay, I'm going to give you a car, the washing machine and dryer, wall-to-wall carpeting, and a good vacuum cleaner. You give me value." Do you understand? That's what we do.

And now, the word *living*. We've established that *relationship* means the condition of retelling our story, and *loving*, which is basically no judgment, very difficult, and the word *living* is an ongoing process of watching and being whatever is the truth. That's what living is. Living is the ongoing process of watching. You see, the truth is available at all times. When you're living, you are in a process of watching and being, watching and being—even that is a relationship. It's two parts. You're watching and you're being whatever is the truth. Now, here's the snag: There's only one place to get the truth, and it's not in your opinion or in anybody else's; it's the source of God within you. It's always the source of God within you. Nothing else is going to give you the truth. Accept no opinions of yourself, including your own. Why? Because you're going to sell yourself short, and I don't know about you, but we can't afford that in my family.

Your Worksheet A

We're going to do a little process to help us look at our relationships, and you're going to choose any one, just pick one. It doesn't have to be one that you have judged as a good one or a bad one. It doesn't mean that you're going to choose a broken-heart story or the love-of-your-life story. It won't matter. You're going to choose one person, and we're going to go through a process that is called the *interview*. First of all, what's an interview? What happens in an interview? You exchange information; there are questions and answers on both sides and you exchange information. Usually the interview concerns what? A job. Here's what I believe. I believe we have subtly interviewed people as they have come into our lives—even our children. You have interviewed these people, and you have actually assigned them jobs that you forgot about, and the problem is two things: The first problem is that the jobs you assigned them may not be the function that God assigned to them in your life, and the second problem is amnesia. So, I want you to choose one person. It doesn't matter whether it's a good relationship, a broken heart, a great relationship, a long-term, a child, a spouse, a mother or father. It doesn't even matter if the person is alive. We're going to reclaim why you hired this person in your life.

- So, if you will, just make yourself comfortable. Put your feet flat on the floor and allow yourself to be in a comfortable position. If you are wearing eyeglasses, it may be helpful for you to take them off just to be more relaxed. Also allow your hands to be loose in your lap, unfolded, not having your arms folded. Loosen it up. And again, we'll begin by having you keep your eyes closed throughout this exercise, and you will begin by breathing in and breathing out, slowly, easily, letting each breath be a little deeper, a little slower than the one before.

- You will allow yourself to really notice your breathing, so you'll fully breathe in and fully exhale out, and while you are breathing you will begin to make the image that this breath you're breathing is actually light. Let it be a cooling blue-white light, a soothing and relaxing blue-white light, and let it move through your whole body. Feel yourself relaxing, and as you are relaxing, repeat several times the following affirmation:

I am learning to live in loving relationships. I am learning to live in loving relationships.

- Repeat this several times, ten times. It's very good to repeat this affirmation. Once you have repeated the affirmation a significant number of times, eight or nine or ten, you will then create an image that you are sitting in a beautiful garden area. Let all of nature be represented, the sound of moving water. In your mind let it be that any persons who sip from the water or wash their faces or hands in this water receive a healing which they may need. The sounds of birds singing, the rustle of the trees' leaves. The temperature is just the right temperature. The season of the year is your favorite season, the sky is clear, and the sun glows in yellow strength. You will then, at the count of three, invite one person to come into this garden with you with whom to learn more about loving relationships. This person will just be with you, and we will then continue to learn more about the interview that happened on a subconscious level the first time you met.

- One, two, three. Sense this person being with you. Sense his or her physical features. Bring back a clear memory of what this person looks like: size, weight, even a special fragrance that he or she might have worn or a special smile. The interview in this exercise represents a subtle exchange of communication that you had with this person that was not spoken verbally but nonverbally, emotionally exchanged. All of us in first meetings make impressions on one another. In the impression, we exchange subtly what we expect from this person, even if it is a newborn child, even if it is the first recollection with your own parents of what you expected a mother or a father to be, or a brother or a sister or a spouse, a friend, a coworker, partner. So just bring to mind some early encounter with this person. See all the images of when you first met. Bring back the feelings of how you felt about this person or about yourself. In fact, include both.

- Notice that there was a subtle assumption or expectation that you might have had about yourself or this person. This is the subtle script that you gave or expected from this person. Sometimes we even expect our children to fulfill the dreams that we did not, or to make us feel important in ways that we did not, to be freer than us, to be more than us. Sometimes we have expectations of our siblings, such as that they should treat us as special because we are of the same blood. We have expectations of spouses, that they should be protectors, that they should be the key one to make us feel valuable and important. We have hidden expectations and subtle impressions that we place upon coworkers, whether they are employees or employers. Let all of this simply come to the surface now, and see it as your initial interview with this person, and then at the count of three ask yourself what you really expected to happen with (mention the person's name).

- One, two, three. What did you really expect would happen with this person? Trust your first impression and know that this may have been a false expectation, a false assumption, and in fact not really the main function as designed by God that really was to be exchanged between you. In a later exercise, we will continue to understand the true lesson as opposed to any false expectations.

- When you are comfortable to do so, open your eyes, and then spend a few moments quietly responding by writing a note or making a mental note of what you felt from this exercise.

What comes out of recalling this interview is that somewhere there may have been a false assumption which is really a condition. It's saying, "I want you to be this for me. You're going to be my everything. You're going to be my security. You're going to be my meal ticket. You're going to be the one who's going to make me feel important. You're going to be the one who is going to be my claim to fame for career." Whatever it might have been, your subconscious said it because you assumed that you needed to be completed by another person. This comes from the normal definition of *relationship*, but the natural definition of *relationship* is not that this person completes you—that says you're not enough—but rather that this person brings out the best in you, merely by the exchange. It's like you are the color blue and somebody else is the color yellow. You remain being blue and the other person remains being yellow, but in the blend of what you share, dynamics, you both get to experience green in a way you've never thought you could. Then the ability to experience green remains with you, not because you need the person to experience green, but because this person helped you to find the green in yourself. Unless we are willing to get rid of the need system in relationships, we will never understand the God function in relationships.

Subtly, the interview was set between you and somebody else—in fact, between you and all the people to whom you relate on a regular basis—and what that does is to make a fixed impression and then start to dictate a script, which leaves no room for growth because now the person is fixed in this mold. Subtly we assign the person a job. "You will be my validator, my rescuer, my bank account, my fan club, my security. You will be my replacement for the family that I didn't have or think I should have had, etc. You will be the person to make me feel important or to get me out into the world in ways that I can't get myself out into the world. You will be my cure for loneliness. You will be my cure for not being able to motivate myself. You will be my motivator."

Now, we do this subtly, and again it doesn't matter who the person is, whether it's a familial, friendly, or work connection. We will do this. Now, what happens is that what is to get exchanged gets kind of fixed. The same way that you're giving a person a script, the other person is also giving you a script. What you've then got is two overlays that are probably not the same, and underneath those two overlays is the truth about why you two are connected and related. The amount of time that the two of you spend together doesn't matter. What is important is that you learn the truth about why you came into each other's lives.

What very often happens is when we give the interview to the person, the other person also gives us an interview. The person doesn't meet the standards, and we fire that person from the job. Then we go out and we find somebody else to fill the job, and then that person doesn't fill the job either, so we fire that person. And that's called *patterns* in relationships. So people will go from job to job, still having the same boss problems. They will go from neighborhood to neighborhood, still having the same neighbor problems. They will continue having problems with relatives. They'll just change the relative. It goes from one kid to a niece to an uncle. They just keep rotating it, but it's the same problem. And they fire the person from the job, and then they hire somebody else. When we say "Attracting the same kind of person," it is a big, red flag that indicates you subtly gave somebody a script in a nonverbal interview.

Again, two people come together, regardless of if it is for a little while, a little longer time, or a very long time, because the two souls are to know each other in a new way of loving the self that they have not been able to find. This does not mean they don't argue or disagree. You have all the emotions that you have, except now they're real, so if you are depressed it's a legitimate depression and not a repressed anger, and if you're happy you're really happy and not just inflated over something that now makes you feel so safe inside or secure when before you weren't. You are much better at identifying your emotions when you follow the natural definition of *relationship*. The natural definition of *relationship* is to see through this person a new way to love you and therefore get closer to loving God, and that can happen when you rub each other the right way as well as the wrong way. Conflict and peace will both bring about the acknowledgment and the awareness that you need to grow closer to the truth about who you are and to get to know who you are as God does, rather than the way that you do. In fact, with conflict you're on the way to peace. With peace maybe there will soon be a new conflict that makes you get to an even greater peace.

So it's not to say that we are removing all struggles from relationships. It's that the struggle has value and it has an end, and the end is peace and deep understanding of how God loves you that could have only come through this person. The person is not special; the love you share is not better than, because it's always God's life you're sharing. When you are with another person and you feel loved, you are sharing God's life. In that, you come to know God's life and power in you, further highlighting your value as a person because you've been able to say to yourself, "The source of God is with me." You're also going to be able to see how through this interaction you learned lots of things that you couldn't have learned by yourself. But this does not ever imply that one person is better than another person. It's just that the exchange is unique. Each exchange that you have with people is unique.

Let's say that this person seems to have identified a pattern in which he keeps going from job to job and having authority problems. He wants to do it one way, and the powers that be say they want it done another way. What is important there is that the person recognizes that the lesson is not about right or wrong but about authority and confrontation, and if this person were to really allow himself to go inside and pray quietly and use one of the exercises that we have described to get in touch with the lesson that he's missing in all these jobs, he would come to understand something. He would uncover that he needed the lesson of confrontation because early in his life he learned that confrontation means losing; because when he was little he was outpowered; because when he was little, when somebody said no it was no, and there was no room for discussion. As an adult, this person goes out into the world, and what he's not aware that he's doing is that he is actually replacing; he's putting his parents into these jobs and authority issues, and he is having a lot of struggle and a lot of conflict about proving his point, that this is the way the job ought to be done. When he leaves the job and goes to the next, it still comes up the same way. The problem is not about the job and the problem is not about being right or wrong. The problem is that this soul is finding parent-like bosses to help the soul resolve one issue, which is that confrontation doesn't mean losing. Confrontation means looking at the word clearly, with the force. It means being able to find the truth and then simply expressing it. But if I have come from a background that says confrontation means I lose, I will become extremely defensive when somebody challenges me, and so I'll fight to be right. I even will be arrogant, overconfident. I will be very defensive, and what I'm really replaying is activity that I wanted to express in childhood or in fact did express in childhood. This is an example of some relationships that are really there to teach us lessons.

In this last exercise, where you revisited the original impression and interview that you had with this particular person, you might have come up with an assumption you had about how this relationship was going to go. What we're going to do in this next interview exercise is redefine the word *interview*, so you can get the truth about the relationship rather than the opinion, expectation, or assumption about it. Unless we are dealing with the truth, we will not experience love. We will experience security swap shop: I need this, you need that; let's see how long we can barter off our goods.

The real definition of the word *interview* comes from the Latin word *inter*, which means "between," and the word *view*, which means "to see." Here's what the new definitions for *relationship* and *interview* are going to look like. I'm drawing a triangle. At the top of the triangle is God. At one base of the triangle is you, regardless of who the you is, and the other base of the triangle is me. This model fits all people, regardless of the form of the relationship. If I am rooted in the apex summit of the triangle, which is God is my source, then there is an arrowhead going from God to me and me to God. The same thing is true—if this person I'm relating to is sourced in God, it will be an exchange. So that when I relate between you and me, I get my answer from the source and channel it. So do you get your answer from the source and channel it. This is the only way to get the truth.

135

TRUE SELF = GOD = SOURCE

Natural Love

↓   Unconditional

Natural
Relationship

YOU _____ ME

_____

_____

Rooted in TRUTH—GOD as Source
allows for real communication,
not making other person the Source/God—
worship as false idol.

_____

YOU _____ ME

Normal Love   Conditional to

↓   Perceptions,

Normal Relationship   Opinions

If I take God out, I'm just exchanging opinions. Regardless of the form of the relationship, if it does not have God as its foundation, which doesn't have anything to do with a religion but has everything to do with identifying that the source of your ability to live and to love is in you already, and the other person is doing the same, the relationship will end because there's no glue. Even if the person dies, moves on, changes because of job, relocation, etc., and you are not in close geographic proximity, the relationship will continue because love is eternal. Once you love, you continue to love. The only thing that changes is the form, which is the relationship. The reason why you love changes. If the relationship stops and the love stops, I will say to you it was not love at all but rather it was the security swap shop.

When you truly love a human being, you do not stop loving that person. You continue to love that person and he or she will continue to love you, even after death. Death has no barrier on love. God is eternal and ever-present. God and love are synonymous. Love is eternal and ever-present, all at the same time. That is why when we really love someone, we experience eternity. We become no longer so mindful of time. A day, a week, a month, ten years, fifteen years go by in a second.

My dearest, closest friends are friends that I made in high school, from the time I was thirteen years old. A week, a month, two months, six months—although we don't let it stretch that far—could go by. We meet again and it's as if nothing changed, because in that I am experiencing God's time. Eternity exists in love. Love is our vehicle, our messenger to get us to experience eternity now, because it is the now. Time could pass, and I could see some of those friends and would be reliving the same laughter we had and living in new laughter and no time was lost whatsoever. Some of my dearest friends are from high school, and I can't even fathom that DECADES have passed since we first met. Where did all those years go? I could get on the phone, and it's as if we were still going to go sit at the lunch table in high school. And time could go by, and it seems like you're not exchanging a whole lot, and then another time passes, and you're exchanging a whole lot of stuff, then you drift apart, and then you come back. That's because once you love, you always love. The only thing that changes is the form of the relationship. The form of the relationship changes according to the lesson. The lesson can only be given to you by God. We're not smart enough to know it on our own. It's got to come from the source.

So if I take God out of the top apex of this, I'm stuck with just an opinion of you, you're stuck with just an opinion of me, and in my opinions I go back to the normal definition of *love* and the normal definition of *security* and that means the normal definition of *relationship*, which is security, and that means I'm going to think I need you. You're going to think you need me to live. We falsify each other as source. We worship false idols in our relationships out of this. But when I understand that God is my source, I become appreciative of you. I become extremely reverent and respectful toward you, because then I know that God assigned you to me for a certain duration in time, whether it is a day, a week, a month, or a lifetime. My mother told me from when I was little that even your children are only on loan. You own no one. Nobody has to be with you. You don't have to be with anybody. It is all by choice and by appointment. Your soul makes the assignments in very subtle ways, and people come to you and you will learn and they will leave. Everybody you have met in your life will leave. Everybody you met in life, you will leave. To ask somebody to be with you forever is insane.

Now, does that say there's no such thing as "until death do us part" and the value and respect of marriage? No. What I'm saying is that even in marriage, even in the best of marriages, somebody goes first, and the strength of the marriage, the beauty in the marriage, is that you grow through the source and know that you are on loan to each other, and you live in the eternity of love now. You appreciate each other now. You have reverence for each other, for each other's bodies, words, emotions, fears, and expectations. It takes a long time to really get to know another person.

Here's the thing about relationships. Relationships are to resemble the truth. The reason for having any relationship at all in life is that what we are to do is to duplicate the way that God loves us in another person. **Now you can't duplicate the way that God loves you until you have figured out how God loves you.** Your primary relationship is to learn how God loves you. Don't assume it and don't expect it in your expectation level, but go in prayer and in silence and let God show you how you are loved. Take the time and the commitment to do that, and then out of that you will learn what love is, and then that's what you have to give to others. I can't love you if I don't know what love is. I will not know what love is until I let the source and Author of Love—that is, God—show me. Once I feel it, I will come to know it, I am free to give it, and then my relationships will soon become the reflection of the way that God loves me. What is missing is that you are not my source, but you are an example of how good God is and how gentle and strong his love is.

So in this exercise of interview we're going to take the same person inside of ourselves, into our mind's eye, but we're going to see the interview as the view between us, and the view between us is God, the real reason for why you were brought together. Again, if I take God out of the triangle, I just have your opinion of me and my opinion of you. It's finite, it's limited, and it's going to cut us both short. When I put God back into the picture where it belongs, now I've got the truth of it, I've got the source of it, and I will know, I will come to know what it is that we are exchanging. People will be with you for a short time, they will be with you for a little longer time, or they will be with you for a very long time. Those are the three styles of relationships: a little bit, a little more, and a lot of bit. The time has nothing to do with it. Why? Because in true love there is no time— there is eternity. When you love, you love forever. Where the person is geographically or planetarily, in what dimension, doesn't matter. Ask people who have loved ones in the next dimension and ask them if they still feel the presence and the caring and the protection when they least expect it and most need it. It's because the love is still binding. It's just not physical. Only one dimension of you is physical. You have many dimensions. You are physical, emotional, mental, and spiritual, and what remains after death is the emotional, mental and spiritual. There is a new body, but it just doesn't look like the one we're sporting now. They come to you in dreams, in impressions, in flashes of insights, in warm feelings of safety, and you will always know that it is them in a particular way. Love doesn't die because God can't die. They are the same.

Your Worksheet B

In this exercise, we're going to use a new definition of *interview*, which is the view between us, which is God's window for why we are together—for a little bit, a little more of bit, and a whole lot of bit—and then out of that you will be able to feel more of the source within you as it connects to all relationships.

- Make yourself comfortable. Allow your feet to be flat on the floor, close your eyes, and again take deep breaths, breathing in and breathing out, slowly and deeply, each breath a little slower and a little deeper. Now allow each breath to be a breath of light, a blue-white light that fills you. Every cell of your body is illuminated in this healing, strong-yet-gentle, blue-white light. As you are allowing your body to fill up in the blue-white light that begins from the center of your chest where you know your heart will be, repeat this affirmation several times quietly, silently, to yourself:

  I see the truth in my relationships. I see the truth in my relationships. I see the true lesson of God's love in all those around me, and it is good.

- And relax.
- Again, picture yourself in that beautiful garden spot, where all of nature is harmoniously represented. Feel the flow of nature, the easiness of it, the goodness of it, the peace of it, the strength that it gives you. Now, at the count of three, you will bring into this garden scene a relationship, the same one that we saw in the first interview. One, two, three. Sense the person as being there. This may be a spouse, a son or daughter, a relative of some kind, a partner, a business colleague, a friend. This person need not be present on this earth plane

at this time. See the person and get a sense of him or her, his or her face and ways. Now at the count of three, bring in the presence of God. Let it be a being of light, or in any symbol that you can relate to as being the Creator. One, two, three. Sense God sitting between the two of you. Rays of God's presence extend to each of you, connecting to you, and then in silence ask, "What is this lesson of love that you have brought me through this person?" and then mention the person's name. Then in silence listen to your first impressions.

- You can repeat this on your own as often as you like. It is also recommended that you would keep a journal of your responses to help you enhance the truth that is being exchanged in the relationships that surround you.

Chapter Eight

We Are All Related

What Happened To Me

Everything I needed to learn, I learned on North Twelfth Street in Newark! As I look back, those were grand, glorious, fearless days. It really was a microscopic view of life. All aspects of life were visible in a one-block radius. Each person was unique, from the four-year-old who died of leukemia, to Mamie who had an adopted daughter, Grace (my first best friend), to Jimmy who had cerebral palsy, to crazy Joe who was the homeless soul we all took care of. I learned from all of them. We all created our neighborhood safety. We wanted to. We made each other safe. We were family.

This part of my life I believe truly built the foundation of belief that we really want to connect to each other and feel safe. My life was rich in alleyways to play in, no locked doors, lots of funny nicknames, and always having someone to play with on Saturdays. We didn't have much money. We didn't notice that till much later. It didn't matter then. We all felt like family.

How You See It

If I say to you we are all related, you would probably have a couple of different responses. One would maybe be a philosophical response where you'd say, "Yes, humanity is connected to humanity," and we can easily identify with that. Shortly after that statement, the connection begins to break down, especially where our own hidden prejudices are concerned. We will then leave that connection and that philosophy and start, if we think of a whole global perspective, dividing humanity into very uneven parts, such as rich and poor, haves and have-nots, educated and uneducated, healthy and not healthy, wealthy and poor, racial discriminations, third world countries. The number of times we could slice this globe as if it were pie is endless, and yet we'll start off by saying, "Oh, yes, humanity is connected to humanity. We are all of the same species. We are all of the same family called humankind."

For me, it is absolutely true that we are related, and I want to take it not from the macro but the micro, so that we can really understand from the smallest fragment and the smallest slice of that pie all the way out to the largest that without a doubt we are connected and we are of the same family.

In the course *The Silva Method*, Jose Silva offers an affirmation that is repeated every exercise, in every meditation, which is prayerful as well as uplifting and so true: "You will connect and relate to all people, to all of humanity, depending upon their ages, as mothers or fathers, brothers or sisters, sons and daughters." That is a very important and powerful statement to make, and that is the truth, that is where the whole vision for peace is moving toward, to be able to know that whoever you are with at work, whoever sits in front of you, behind you, beside you on a bus, whoever is in a movie line, a bank line, is truly a kindred spirit and a family member.

This brings up another question, or maybe even another problem. We don't get along with our own micro families, and in some cases it's easier to identify with this large family because it's not so intimate. It's much easier. We don't have to deal with the same stuff, and many times people will say, "My friends connect and treat me better; my coworkers connect and treat me better than my own blood," and other people will say the opposite. Other people will have another prejudice and they will say, "Well, you know, we're not family."

If this were my grandmother, no matter who you were she would make you a relative. Even if she just met you, she would start to question you in such a way that it would almost sound like an inquisition, and she'd say, "Where do you live? Where are you from?" And anyone within a hundred and fifty mile radius of New York she would make a relative. She would say, "Wait a minute, wasn't your father friends with Sam Garuta who used to have the sausage store on Fourth Street? Upstairs he had rooms" (not an apartment—rooms, with a parlor and a sun porch. We don't use these words anymore). And she would say, "Yeah, the man upstairs, Angelo, I knew him. I knew we were related." She would go round about in any way possible, and I didn't understand that because, as I was growing up, I used to say, "Nana, what are you doing? You don't know him," and she'd say "Sssh" and she'd give me one of these elbow pokes, you know. But what she was doing was establishing some common denominator, and she would go to any length to do it, so that she would have a familial connection as she spoke with you.

My grandmother's name was Mary and her nickname was Mary Ma. Everybody in the neighborhood knew her as Mary Ma. There was always somebody living in the house who really wasn't a relative, but Mary Ma was helping out because she worked with this young man's mother and now he's just getting married, he just came out of the service, he doesn't have enough money to get married, so Nickie boy is now going to live with Mary Ma for six months, and she's going to take all his money and hold onto it. She's going to give it all back to him in six months so he can start a life, and she did this for more people in the neighborhood.

In fact, where I grew up in Newark we called everybody aunt and uncle, and I had no idea that they were not blood. There was Uncle Tony and Aunt Sara across the street. They lived downstairs from my maternal grandparents. We lived upstairs from my paternal grandparents. Next door was Aunt Eleanor and Uncle Mike. They're not related. One day my mother said to me, "You know, Uncle Mike is not your real uncle, but Mommy just taught you to say that out of respect." I was about fifteen. This was like a culture shock. I had an identity crisis over this. "They're not—what do you mean they're not really blood?" I was taught to say that anybody who was on that block was an aunt or an uncle or a cousin, and what did I know? I thought my family invested in real estate, had bought the block. I had no idea. This is just what you did.

I don't remember locked doors. I remember going in the alleyway and the big deal was that I was going to go two houses down to go and play with my friend Gracie, and between alleys the mothers would watch from the stoop, but I thought I was out in freedom land because I was walking two houses away.

There was also a little method to this relative thing, because there was always a pair of eyes watching out for you. There was always somebody around the corner. The door was open. If you needed something, you would go into the house. I can remember my mother saying to me, "Go by Mamie." There was a whole set of names that never came up in history again. Gilda, Mamie—you don't repeat these names and I don't know where they come from, but they don't happen again. There was never a Danielle in 1950. So you would go to Mamie's house and the door would be open, and whatever you had to borrow you had to borrow, and then in the process would go an extra piece of something, a newspaper clipping, whatever she borrowed, buttons. "Here, I got these extra buttons. Bring them back to your mother because she sews."

Sunday night was a big deal. My mother and father had their first television, a nine-inch TV, on Twelfth Street. Now we went from small televisions to huge televisions, back to small televisions, soon to TV that's on the face of a watch. Well, they had this nine-inch television, thirty-two people jammed into my mother's living room, which was only comfortable to fit about five, and we watched the *Ed Sullivan Show*, and before we did that everybody had to eat. Somebody had the eggs, somebody had the milk and somebody had the pasta; somebody had cheese and somebody had homemade wine. They had fettuccini Alfredo because it was cheap and it stuck to your ribs and it was protein, and now we call it a delicacy and you can get a half order for $9.95. This is what I understood growing up, and I think it's connected sometimes more to city than suburban living. What happened in suburbia is that we separated. The fences went up. The lawns got wider and longer, sometimes not even greener, in between the houses. If you wanted to play as a kid, you had to be driven, you had to be picked up. You were isolated.

Saturday morning on North Twelfth Street was a party. You would simply get up and walk outside, and there was somebody to play stick ball, hopscotch, punch ball, three flies up, anything at all that you wanted to play, not because we had toys (batteries not included). We had chalk, we had jump-rope, we had a wagon, and my favorite all-time toy, to this day even, is a refrigerator box. We watched and watched for somebody in the neighborhood to get a main appliance in their house, and we would go and do all kinds of favors to be the first kids to have dibs on this refrigerator box, because we'd go inside the box and we'd cut windows and we'd draw flowers, and then when we got tired of that we'd roll in it, and we would pray that it wouldn't rain so we could go out the next day and the next week, until finally the weather had the better part of this refrigerator box. Then we waited for the next Maytag repairman to come and say "I'm sorry, Mrs. Carcillo, you need a new refrigerator."

That's what I remember. There was an available element that allowed us to connect to each other. People who were raised in cities, whether it was Newark or New York City or Chicago, any major metropolitan area where people had to live close together for some reason or other, argued and got over it. They shared. They all had problems. Everybody had to work hard. Nobody had enough on their own, but somehow together, whoever chipped in, you had more because of the neighborhood. If you needed a shoemaker, you went to Uncle Mikey's son because, poor thing, he's just starting a business. You needed veal cutlets, you wanted them sliced thin, go to Johnnie boy. He's now fifty-three, by the way, and still slicing meat real thin. All of this was based on the fact that people knew that they needed each other in one way or another.

Then the sixties happened. Then drugs happened. Then "God is dead"[41] happened. We just became anesthetized and drew pictures on Volkswagen vans and dropped out of society because there was a second phase of an industrial revolution happening, which was making us separate more and more from each other, making it harder and harder for us to relate, making it harder and harder for us to support a family economically. For the first time, it was keeping up with the Joneses. In the fifties, the Joneses lived with you because they couldn't afford anything either. After that, it was who had bigger and better and more, and this whole consumption function that echoed over the next several decades has now made us afraid of each other. When we become afraid of each other, we will breed separation. **Separation invites violence.** We can't trust each other.

The neighborhood grocery store was the first charge account and credit line where people would go in and say they needed eggs, they needed meat, they needed this, they needed that, "Catch you at the end of the week." The owner had an old book that looked like the

---

[41] Jean-Paul Sartre, *Existentialism and Human Emotions* (New York: Wisdom Library, 1957), 15.

old-fashioned black and white composition book, and a broken pencil that he shaved the tip of with a pen knife because he didn't even have a pencil sharpener, and he wrote it all down by first name. "Bobby boy, four eggs." And that's how we lived. Nobody had, but if there was a problem, everybody showed up. If there was somebody sick, everybody showed up.

When I think of that slice of life that was on that block, North Twelfth Street in Newark, every element of life was represented. You know that book, *Everything I Needed to Know I Learned in Kindergarten?* Well, I could probably write my own version: *Everything I Needed to Learn I Learned from 433 North Twelfth Street.* We had Crazy Joe. What was he? He was the homeless guy. Everybody knew he was a little off—he probably had Alzheimer's. Everybody watched him and took care of him, and he hung out outside of St. Francis Church, where the nuns fed him. He was harmless. He just stayed around. As a kid, I remember seeing him out in the school yard. "Hey, Crazy Joe." We used to call him that to his face. "Yo, Crazy Joe, how ya doing? What's happening?" But it was harmless.

Across the street we had Jimmy, who was born with cerebral palsy. We would always make sure that he was on first base when we would play, because most of us couldn't hit anyway and so we made a big deal that Jimmy was on first base, and he'd just fall. He would just fall and save the day and no matter who went past him, "No, Jimmy caught it." He couldn't catch. He couldn't even open his hands. He had an impaired gait on one side and his hands were closed, but we made sure that these people were part of the team. Some of them are still even living there.

Then there was Jessica. Jessica was Jimmy's older sister. Jessica got pregnant before she was married and she is the original "beauty school dropout" from *Grease.* Nobody said anything, and I remember the baby and I remember how everybody was excited and they all threw a shower and they all gave baby clothes, everything. I remember that. What did I know? "Mommy, why is she getting that baby?"

"Shut up." That was the response. "But, Ma, is she eating too much?" "Shut up, I told you, and don't bring it up in front of her." This was dysfunctional family dynamics. There was one phrase: "Shut up." But I learned from that, whatever it was, that it was very clear that I was not to bring this up.

Down the street, we had Barbara Corolla. Little Barbara Corolla was four years old and she had leukemia. She died of leukemia. Her mother took all the kids in the neighborhood—I'm talking about maybe twenty kids—to the house and explained to us what this was and told us that Barbara was very special. I remember this. At fifty-two years old, forty-five years later, I remember this exactly, that I could see the porcelain sink—those big clunky porcelain sinks. Roper, I think, was the name of the stove. You can't see them now unless you watch *American Movie Classics*. That's the only place you're going to see those sinks and those stoves. I can remember the mother took us in and she explained to us that Barbara went to Heaven because she was really a special angel, and that she was sent to us so that we would know what an angel looked like and we would come to appreciate angels and children better. Barbara had strawberry blond hair and blue eyes, and she was a very delicate little child; I remember knowing that this was okay. It's good to be an angel. Because we were around Barbara, they let us go to the wake if we wanted to. I wanted to go and my brother didn't. They put all the lights on in the funeral home. They made it all open. They moved all the chairs out. They had everybody come in and they said that she was sleeping. They had her dressed up. And I came home and I said, "Mommy, Barbara went to a party because I saw her dress." This is just what I learned. I didn't know anything else.

I'm only trying to make the point that we were not afraid of each other, and there were problems just like anything else. We had people who lost their jobs and I got the same response. "Ma, how come Uncle Louie's home again?" "Shut up. He's helping your father." And it was just, "Well, okay, this is what it is." There was something about the acceptance that life has problems and we band together. That's the important part in all walks of life.

My brother was six years old and playing the piano, and he had a friend down the street, Richie Greco. My brother had one piano lesson and Richie had one trumpet lesson and they were starting a band. They were horrible.

I remember the young boy Bruce who lived down the street in an old Army barracks because the family couldn't afford anything else. Who were they? They were welfare people. "Ma, how come there's no curtains on their house?" "Shut up. Just go bring these to his mother"—curtains that my mother made to go and bring, which were made out of some extra tablecloths or God knows what—"and just tell the mother that we had extra, we don't need these, and if she doesn't want them, it's okay." And what was I learning? That we had plenty. None of us had enough, but you made do. There was a creativity of bonding. There was a creativity of knowing if you lived in this small radius, that was your turf. That was your territory. That was what you were to take care of. I would never think of going off the block. To me there was no life outside of my block. What did I know?

Then we moved. We moved to the suburbs, and I lost that sense of going out and being able just to be free and just go in and out, up and down stoops, and three-family houses and four-family houses, and I remember making an adjustment in my own mind that my sanctuary now was not on a stoop. On two or three sides, my house was surrounded by woods, and so the highlight of my playground now was not the alleyway but the woods, and we had the constant project of building the best tree fort we could, with whatever kids were available—and there weren't many. And I remember even as young as eight years old I continued to go where I was raised, because we went to see our grandparents. It was a Sunday ritual. You went to see one set of grandparents, then you went to see the other. You ate all day. You went up and down the street. Now we're going to Aunt

Sarah's, and now over here, and Louis and Lena Maligio. You can't make these names up. They don't have them anymore. Look in the phone book. You're not going to find them anymore.

So I continued to do this until another ten-whatever years, and I watched this change, you see, and little did I know that maybe the pictures that I was recording were about how life was changing right before my eyes. You watched life change in your own neighborhood in your own way. We all have stories. This is just mine. There were problems. There were fights. There were arguments. There were children who died, and somebody was crippled and somebody was out of work, and somebody left his wife. It was all represented, but the main element is that we were not afraid of each other, and that is because each family continued to bring that element to their children, and then to their children's children, to say "this is the neighborhood."

Look at what is happening now. We're having a kind of flashback in a new way. The sixties, as I said, isolated us in suburbia. It separated us all, and even for a kid to play on the little league he has to have equipment and he's got to have a physical and a permission slip and an insurance form. Where's the fun? Where's the fun for this kid to just go and knock the ball around and not care about whether he's the best player or not? Where's the fun in just getting dirty in the dirt and coming home and knowing that you hung out with some kids and that they were your team, and not caring who won the game? You know, we made the sewer first base and the manhole cover second, the other sewer third, and the pizza place home. So we found it; you always find it. And we had like maybe two mitts and we kept passing them. As the ball went out, we'd throw a mitt to the kid in center field to "Hurry up and put it on, here"! They'd catch the mitt and try to catch the ball. This was quite a feat of acrobatics, let alone the fact that everybody had to have his or her own equipment. We didn't have enough equipment to go around for everybody.

But it was more about people connecting. Those were your brothers and sisters, you see. Then we got to the seventies and we got to this horrible, please spare me, *me generation*, where everybody wanted to be who they already were, and they pushed for their rights and pushed for their rights, and in some ways, yes, there were very positive effects, but the neighborhood connection and the familial community was dying year after year. Then in the eighties it got worse because we got greedy. We built big, enormous homes that we couldn't afford to heat in the winter and keep cool in the summer. By the time you had enough money to pay for this monstrosity, all your kids moved out and now whoever it was that you were living with was a total stranger and you didn't even know how to talk to that person.

And now we're in a new century. We are economically broken. We are emotionally distant and frightened. We have a hole in our soul, because we can't find peace, nor God, or justice. Why is it that we still can't get this right? We have twenty years of literature about dysfunctional families, and we still can't see the light of day. We're starting to try to get back to this. You see the news in New York with the coffee shops. What are they eliminating? Booze, number one, and darkness. People are meeting and talking in coffee shops. I mean, how sobering and cerebral, with lights on, and people standing up and reciting poetry; it is amazing that this is happening. They're springing up like crazy, and why are people going there? To hang out. That's not what they're saying, but that's what they need, and that's what they're trying to do. If you talk to any person who may not be married any longer or yet, or with a partner or a family, there's no place to convene with people.

There's no place for kids. After grade school, there's no place for high school and college kids. There's no place for them to hang out in a safe and protected environment. It's dangerous. You know, I would not want to go back and be a teenager now. In fact, I just said to some of my friends with whom I went to high school that now, at fifty-two years old, I feel emotionally confident enough to go away to college. Nearly forty years have passed, and I think I could now handle going away to college! College was horrendous for me, not only because of my learning disabilities at the time, but because there was no connection, not unless it was sex, drugs, and rock and roll. There was no connection. There was no place to just be with people and tell your stories. Whenever my cousins, family, or anybody from that neighborhood element meet at some kind of reunion, somebody's fiftieth wedding anniversary, some wake, some kid getting married, some grandchild of that neighborhood setting, they tell the same stories all over again, and I watch the aliveness and the light in their faces for telling the story again about the ability to connect.

You will hear people say over and over, "Those were the good old days," yet the truth is nobody wants to go back to the poverty, the lack of conveniences and technology. Yes, I don't want to go back to that either. But what we want to have some way to bring forward is that ability to connect to each other as a family. That is what we are sorely missing. We're desperately missing community. What has happened over the last thirty or forty years since then is this element of repeated separation, generation after generation of separation, where families don't even really sit down to a meal anymore and relax and be with each other. They don't do that. We have fast foods, we have fast quick everything, and what we are repeating in the micro, which is our nucleus, our family, our spouses, our partners, our kids, nieces, nephews, or cousins, is a thought pattern.

We believe that there is a genetic perpetuation of biology, meaning that from generation to generation you could be born with a genetic propensity for something, such as diabetes, heart disease, high blood pressure. We even have statistics now showing that abuse, alcoholism, substance abuse, and other ailments are influenced genetically. We know that biologically we inherit. This, I believe, is where we need to make what is known as—you may have heard of this expression—a *paradigm shift*. A paradigm is a model that we follow, not because it is inherently good or bad, positive or negative, but because it just is the first and we follow it. It's an idea that catches on and we follow it. There was a paradigm fifty years ago in cities as there was a paradigm in rural areas about family, and so that got handed down generation to generation, and then there was a shift and it got out of that.

In the sixties, through the suburbs there was a paradigm shift of community and neighborhood that was not about a togetherness, but about isolation and separateness. It was about more economics. It was about a matter of finances and not a matter of heart and needs and sharing. This got repeated, and what we are now understanding is that that also created an ongoing energy inheritance. We have generations now of dysfunctionality, and fifty years ago there were the same problems as the ones we see now. We still had abuse, we had alcohol, we had violence, we had rape, we had crime, and part of the reason why it is so predominant in our culture is because we are more heavily populated, and also because of the communication network it is talked about more.

What It Really Is

The communication has its positives and its negatives. It is positive in that people are learning about how all this separation and violence is hurting us and how we have to take a stand and have a responsibility to stop it. It is negative in that the more that energy goes out, the more we will get stuck in this dysfunctionality. I believe that the neighborhood of the fifties and sixties prepared the groundwork for a great shift in who we really are. We moved quickly after those years into fast-paced revolutionary awareness that opened up so many layers of our nature. New information and insights gave us knowledge and hope to halt our dysfunctional ways. We are conscious enough, we are alert enough, we are aware enough to be able to stop it. There's more material out now that is going to be able to help us.[42]

Let me explain a little bit more about what a paradigm is.[43] If you went to a hotel and it had sixteen floors and you got in the elevator and wanted to go to the fifteenth floor, you'd push number fifteen and you'd watch the elevator go up—eighth floor, ninth, tenth, eleventh, twelfth floor, then fourteenth floor, fifteenth, etc. Why don't many elevators have thirteenth floors? Because of a superstition. Is a superstition based on truth? Don't we all know that it is based on something that is illogical and an illusion and a falsehood? Yet that paradigm about the thirteenth floor is so strong that architects will build it into their hotels all around the world. That is a paradigm, since it is accepted as normal.

What we have accepted as normal now is that we are dysfunctional, that families are unhealthy and diseased emotionally. That's the attitudinal paradigm, and the biological paradigm is that we have to live with sickness and that it is a power outside of us that will probably be victorious over us. You and I can change both, and it will begin when we understand a single new paradigm of a family.

The new paradigm, as I am suggesting, begins not with the biological mother or father that you had, but from an understanding of the mother principle and the father principle. These are universal

---

[42] Adult Children of Alcoholics   John Bradshaw Workshops
      Al-Anon/Alateen   Deepak Chopra Workshops
      Alcoholics Anonymous   Marianne Williamson
      Co-Dependents Anonymous   Workshops
      Debtors Anonymous   The Institute of Poetic Sciences
      Emotions Anonymous   The John E. Fetzer Institute
      Gamblers Anonymous   The Spindrift Foundation
      Narcotics Anonymous   The Silva Method International
      Overeaters Anonymous
      Sexaholics Anonymous

[43] *Par-a-digm*, n. an example; a model to follow, given.

concepts. These are very much equal to what Carl Jung called *archetypes*.[44] Jung believed that there are about twenty-two archetypes innately imprinted within us in a collective unconscious, and they are equal to the perfect form. He names them as authority, justice, law, peace, love, God, mother, father, friend, to list a few. He says also that there is in us a universal intelligence that connects us and makes us all a family, and that the idea of a perfect mother or father or brother or sister or justice or authority or peace is innately in us. As sure as you are breathing, you are breathing that universal intelligence, you are breathing that Creator's life, and that Creator's life is the perfect form of these concepts. He says that they are imprinted in us, and that part of the conflict that we have in life is that we innately know what a mother or father is supposed to be. I'm just focusing on those two, because I want to make a point about how the micro in this new paradigm shift of attitude plus biology can change the macro family, and you and I can do this; it doesn't have to take another generation to get the job done.

The mother principle was described by Carl Jung and also by other people who understand this universal intelligence, who understand the metaphysics of the within, such as Ernest Holmes from Science of Mind. Deepak Chopra also speaks about the innate intelligence within us to draw upon the mother-father principles within us. The mother principle in us is equal to our innate ability already to have unconditional love.

The father principle is the innate ability that we already have to know what the law of cause and effect is. These two ideas are, in fact, exactly equal to what Carl Jung called the main elements of who we are at a spiritual level, which is the *animus* and the *anima*. The animus is male energy, father energy, and projected energy. So when I understand animus energy in me, regardless of my gender, I will

---

44   Anthony Stevens, Ph.D., *Archetypes* (New York: William Morrow, 1982), 29-30, 39-40.

understand a true concept of father, I will understand a true concept of male, and I will understand a true concept of the law of cause and effect, which is male, and then I will understand that what I send out is what comes back to me. I will understand that what I say is what is going to become my personal reality. This is an animus concept. This is a male energy concept. This is a father concept.

Now, what does this have to do with your father? If we only have an old paradigm of father, we will all stay dysfunctional because there is no perfect father, but the father you got was to start you to unravel the process of coming to understand male energy, animus energy, projective energy, building energy out in the world, to get you to understand that part of your life is to live in the law of cause and effect, to get you to be responsible for your words and your actions. Now, in some cases your father did teach you this, and in other cases your own biological father in fact did not teach you this.

In this new paradigm shift that I'm talking about, when you understand the energy of animus, which is already in you, you will be able to have the true form of father, animus, and male. You will be able to have a true understanding of cause and effect, and it will be easier for you to see your own father, your own biological father, and see him for a man who is on the planet learning lessons that may or may not be similar to yours, and he is not perfect, nor has he ever been perfect. You will be able to see from this man, whether you were adopted or not, that this man started a process of getting you to go deeper into your own self and find the archetype and find how to become more responsible to the law of cause and effect, because it is a universal law that we all must live by. When you can go inside and see in the energy, the intelligence, the universal God-like intelligence within you, that that energy is in one aspect a male energy and a father, you'll begin to father yourself. You will no longer harbor the resentment and the pain that your biological father may or may not have created the dynamics for you in your childhood. You will be able to separate away, in fact, from the biological father, and it will become easier to forgive him because he is only a man and not the full embodiment of the father principle that you already have within you.

The mother principle in you already is the universal intelligence inside of you, already coded in you, about unconditional love. The mother you had may or may not have been unconditional. When you learn to see your mother as a woman who for better or worse brought you into the world and became an example that sparked how to get you again to go within yourself and learn about anima energy— which is female, receptive, intuitive, prayerful, and learning to trust your instincts—when you can learn that mother God principle from within you, you will let go of putting mother on a pedestal and stop asking of her to give you value in your life, regardless of your gender. You will seek inside for your own value, because within you is the archetype; imprinted on your soul is a mother God imprint. Within you is the anima that will always love you and always nurture you. It will be filled with wisdom, and at that point you will begin to mother yourself. Again, you'll be able to forgive your mother and see her as a woman who came into this life bearing her own needs and wounds of the heart, and who was less capable of plowing through those problems than we are because there weren't twenty years of self-development books on the shelves for her to go to like there are for you and me.

We have got to shift the paradigm that says we are dysfunctional. I will declare a moratorium on *dysfunctionality*. I am tired of the word. I am tired of the word *codependent*. I am tired of the excuse that we are not upright and happy and living and breathing joyous people because of what our mothers or fathers did or didn't do. They are not God, and they are not to be worshipped as false pagan idols. They brought you into this earth and they gave you the best that they could, wounded in their own way.

Our responsibility is to take this new model, this new example, this new paradigm, and say the archetype, the true image of what a loving mother and what a cause-and-effect responsible father is, is in me, because the power of God is there and that is my source. Whatever happened to you in your childhood did happen, but you are alive and you are breathing and what you must declare is your own personal victory, that you—no matter how bad it was—are out of it. But now you, as a human being, must exercise the greatest power that you have been given, which is the power of choice. You must choose to stop dysfunctionality. You must choose to stop codependency now. You must stop blaming life, the world, your mother, your father, authority, economics, the size of your house, the number of toys, the amount of money or education. You must stop blaming and go within. Seek first the kingdom of Heaven and everything else shall be revealed to you.

This is not a theory. This is a law of life that was told two thousand years ago. It was told four thousand years ago from the lawgiver Moses. It was taught six thousand years ago from the Buddhist theory of cause and effect.

In this modern age, we must act on what we know. Everybody already knows more than what they're using. **You know enough. Act on it.** We must acknowledge—that's the word I use—the power that we have. That means I take the knowledge that I have within me and I act on it. We are a lazy society emotionally. We are babies emotionally. I think of my grandparents—and maybe this is the same for some of you, for all of us—who came from another country, not even speaking the language, got on a boat with chickens and goats and God knows what else, and came to another country and started a business at fifteen years old and raised a family. We're on the third generation of a business that started from my grandfather at the turn of the century, which has supported the kids and grandchildren and great-grandchildren, and put them through school, bought them boats and cars and houses. This came from Dominic and Angelina, who couldn't even speak English, but came and had a conviction of life in them.

159

We are the weaker race. We are the weaker generation—not mentally, but emotionally. This is the most phobic society that we have had in thousands of years. We've got an excuse for absolutely everything. We have a syndrome for absolutely everything. We have a medication for absolutely everything.[45] And what I believe is the power of God within you is calling you. Every time you take a breath, the power of God is saying to you, "Come to me. I will give you peace and strength and wisdom." But that power is unconditional and cannot drag you in, and what happens typically to us is that we will have crises in our families, and very often the crisis in the family is what will be the huge wake-up call for the family. Bernie Siegel talks about this in *Love, Medicine and Miracles*,[46] and in the second book of *Peace, Love and Healing*, where he says many times that when there is somebody who has a terminal illness, it is then and only then that

---

[45] Stanton Peele, *Diseasing of America* (Boston, MA: Houghton Mifflin, 1989), 15.

> It is fairly clear that medical and pharmaceutical breakthroughs on the level of the antibiotics in the case of first-generation diseases have not been forthcoming in dealing with our major illnesses. While nearly all physicians endorse the use of psychotropic drugs for these conditions, hardly any regard them as a cure and nearly all recognize that they work only irregularly and produce serious side effects and few benefits for at least some patients suffering from conditions under attack. What is more, there is a residual uneasiness about making patients depend on drugs (and the medical approach requires them to do so for the rest of their lives) when benefits are so variable and when some people do as well without them.

[46] Bernie S. Siegel, M.D., *Love, Medicine and Miracles* (New York: Harper and Row, 1986), 138.

family is finally talking about emotions and finally banding together and pulling together.[47]

What I say is stop having the crises. Don't wait for a crisis. Be the mother and father to yourself now. We've got to grow up. We've got to stop making the excuses. We've got to reach inside in daily prayer, in daily exercise, and make the paradigm shift first in attitude. The paradigm shift for attitude is this: "I am a child of God and the power within me is greater than me. From this, all things are made possible."

That is the paradigm shift. That is what will stop dysfunctionality. How many more times must we hear on the news about another domestic fight, another domestic act of violence? Eighty percent of police calls are for domestic violence; whether they are physical or emotional, we've got to stop the pain because we are all related. The power of God is within you and God is your mother and God is your father, and we must draw upon that perfect image of mother and father and know we are safe. Out of that, we will be able to build, in the twenty-first century, a renewed community with all its technology minus the fear. We will be able to come together and celebrate and be of service.

In the seventies and eighties, people pulled together out of desperation in some very helpful organizations, but some of them may have gotten off the track, such as codependent groups and NA and AA—not that they are wrong. They are good and they are positive and they have literally helped millions, but many times

---

[47] Bernie S. Siegel, *Peace, Love and Healing* (New York: Harper and Row, 1989), 166-167. The following is an excerpt from "How to Stay Well":

> Create fun, loving, honest relationships allowing for the expression and fulfillment of needs for intimacy and security. Try to heal any wounds in past relationships, such as with old lovers and mother and father.

people went there because it was the only place for them to connect and it became a culture within a culture.[48] It became a subculture of safety. We even poke fun at them: "Oh, yeah, he's a twelve-stepper. Just listen to him"; "Me, I'm into group"; and so forth.

We cannot do that anymore. In the twenty-first century, what we must do is branch out in service and celebration. We must be able to take the attitude of the past that says, "I have the noodles and you have the butter and you have the eggs and I got the wine and you got the bread, and twenty of us are going to come and boil water and eat, and then what we're going to do is we're going to raise money and build and we're going to help the children. We're going to help all the prejudices of the world, and we're going to have the activities." We've got to take the power back in our hands. And the two key words are *service* and *celebration*. Service is not to be of a victimizing feeling or of a pressure of a woe-is-me. It's going to be about celebrating. So that when you come together, you come together out of abundance and you give because you already have, and out of this you will draw closer together.

The people of the rural communities knew this. They called it the barn-raising activity. We have to have a barn-raising activity where everybody in the neighborhood comes together and literally builds somebody's house. That's what we have to do in the twenty-first century. That is the macro influence, but first we've got to take care of the micro—and get rid of the personal fear—so that we can be a better civilization.

Your Worksheet A

We're going to do an exercise now that's going to help you to shift your own paradigm, which means something that you got stuck in your head about what your mother is and about what your father is,

---

[48]   See note 2.

and we're going to go through an exercise so that you can claim back the right to be your own mother and your own father, knowing that it is a mother God and a father God that breathes within you. This will help you break the chains of guilt, fear, and victimization.

- Allow yourself to be comfortable. If you wear eyeglasses, it's probably better if you take them off. I'm going to ask that you be in a sitting position, upright and alert. If for some reason you repeat this later on and you need to lie down, I would say okay, lie down, but be certain that your shoulders and neck and head are supported slightly at an angle, since this will help you to maintain your consciousness. We want you awake and alert while you're resting and while you're going to an inner level where the true power that you are, that true human potential, is waiting. All you need to do is keep your eyes closed through this exercise and breathe easily and deeply, in a rhythmic manner.

- Close your eyes and take a deep breath and, relaxing now, begin to make each breath a little deeper, a little slower, a little easier. It is very helpful for you to repeat the word *relax* to yourself as you are breathing in and out. As you continue to breathe, breathe in light. Let it be a golden light. Let it be in a playful and even childlike manner that you're breathing in sunshine, exhaling sunshine, so that you can feel it radiating from the center of your chest, radiating through every pore and every fiber of your body. Relax and go deeper and go deeper.

- Relax and go deeper. Feel the energy flowing through you, gently massaging and relaxing your scalp and your neck, your shoulders and your arms, even through to your fingertips. Feel a glowing warmth and a healing inside your chest, especially around your heart. Feel it down your spine, in your hips, all the way down your legs, thighs, knees, calves, shins, ankles, and feet. Relax and continue to follow with me in your imagination.

- As I count from one to three, you will imagine that you are in a beautiful garden. Let all of nature be represented there. One, two, three. Sense being fully there, free and radiant, glowing in sunshine. Let all of nature be represented—the sound of moving water, a tranquil and vast open blue sky, the sunlight stretching down and dressing you in garments of golden string, a smooth and easy breeze moving across you, cleansing your mind, your thoughts of all fear, of all anger, of all resentment, of all pain, of all hurt, and of all insecurities. Fragrance of flowers; the magnificent rainbow colors are represented in these flowers; and you are in this beautiful garden place, an open meadow, feeling good just to be who you are right here and right now.

- At the count of three, you will bring into this scene your mother. One, two, three. Bring into the scene now, in this garden, your mother. Recreate a picture of her, even if she is already deceased and in the next dimension. Really sense her being in front of you. Notice the character of her face, the color of her hair, her eyes. If you need clarification, just imagine that you have a magnifying glass or a focus lens that will help you to see more clearly. You are using your imagination. You are bringing back a memory, a picture of your mother. Sense her physical body, her weight, her shape, her characteristics, her smile, her hands. Sense her in a familiar activity—at work, cooking, driving, in the garden outside of the home—and begin to think of her as a woman, not as your mother but just as a woman. Begin to think of where this woman came from in terms of her own history, her childhood, her background, her talents, her fears, her pain. Any memory will serve the purpose for this healing. Think of your own personal relationship with your mother. It may have a combination of happy and hurtful memories.

- Now sense the golden light inside of you. This golden light contains in it the true mother principle. You already know what it is to have a nurturing, unconditional mother love pour out of you, for it is God the mother within you who teaches you. Your biological mother, whether in positive or negative ways, was given to you to start the process of coming to learn what true love and true nurturing and true faith and trust really are. She was not perfect, is not perfect, but the mother God within you is. Draw from within whenever you need to learn about unconditional love, about nurturing, about faith, about intuition, from the mother God within you, and then see your own mother as the woman in your life who began this process for better or worse. It is up to you to exercise your birthright by choosing to learn about mothering, about mother love, about female love, from the mother God, the female God within you. Be still now and listen to that still voice inside of you and trust your very first impressions as you ask, "What is it that my heart was to learn from this woman whom I call mother?" Be still and listen and trust in the God within you.

- Relax. Later you will reflect on these first impressions. Still sensing the sunshine light within you, still identifying that power of light within you as God, see the woman you called mother sitting by your side and now be ready, at the count of three, to bring into the scene your father. Again it is irrelevant if your father is deceased and moved to the next dimension, whether you have had a good relationship with him or not, whether you are adopted or not. Bring whomever you consider to be your father. One, two, three. Begin to focus on this man whom you call father—his face, his eyes, the structure of his body, his hands. See him in some familiar activity—working with tools or at a desk, with the family, reading, any fatherly, typical activity that you saw this man engaged in.

- Begin to think of your own personal relationship with this man whom you call father. Think of his talents and where he came from, his own story, his own history, whatever it is that he had to overcome in his life. Think of your own personal interaction and relationship with him, the combination of the positives and the negatives, the happy memories and the hurtful ones, and then focus directly on the light in your heart, that golden sunshine light that is in your heart, and know that this is God. This is the father God within you, and within you already is the innate intelligence, the innate power to know what a father love is, to know deep inside of you what it is to live a life according to the law of cause and effect, and that this man you call father was there to start the process of teaching you the law of cause and effect. Understanding that for better or worse he was a man, just a man, imperfect and not God, and that the God within you is the source of law will teach you how to be projective out in the world, how to be creative and dynamic and assertive and confident out into the world, how to truly keep your word and be responsible to your own word, how to make law in your life by learning the law of cause and effect. This man whom you call father started the process and you now must exercise your birthright and choose to go within to the father God and be set free to be productive and constructive and confident and assertive out in the world, living by the law that is God. See him now in this light and relax.

- See your father to the other side of you, so that the woman you call mother and the man you call father are standing at your side and in the center is you, and you are radiant in sunshine. And so, too, they are radiant in sunshine, because they too are children of God and they too have the full power of God within them, and they may or may not be choosing to exercise the power, but you can choose now. Look to first the mother and then the father. Forgive and forget, and with the full power of that God light within you, walk forward into the life that you truly want to live.

- Begin now to see the life you want to live with your family, with your friends, with your coworkers, with your spouse, with your partners. See the celebration go forward, but feel the sunshine as the source of God who keeps you safe, who both mothers you and fathers you through all time. In this light, all is healed, all is made possible. Walk away from the past by choosing in the present to act with the power of God. In this, you are promised a bright future that will lead this next generation in peace. Amen.

- Relax, and when you are comfortable to do so, please open your eyes and remain quiet for just a few moments to give you time to reflect on these thoughts and feelings.

Following from this mother-father principle, what we're doing is changing. What we typically do is see our sense of growth and development from a pathology, which means we usually see the way that we grow up and the way that we develop in life, both physically and emotionally, from a perspective of what was missing, what was wrong. This actually becomes recorded in the consciousness. It actually gets written, stamped on the engrams, which are the nerve cells in your brain, and you are guaranteed to repeat the problems, because the brain functions like a bioplasmic computer. Based on the age-old cliché, "First impressions are lasting," what happens is the first impression of the dynamics of the family get stamped in and what we have then is an imprint of dysfunctionality and an ideal of how to function in life based on our goals and our ideas, which will always clash.

By starting from a mother-father principle, I am dealing with the raw energy that you are, which is your power. The biology where you came from is only a manifestation of that energy, so in the same way I'm going to continue to go through a growth stage that's based on what's right about you and not what is wrong about you. There's so much focus on how we have been crippled and limited that we are literally perpetuating the fact that history repeats itself. We're making history repeat itself. When I start from the shift that says the power of God is within me, the power of God is the full concept of mother-father, is the full concept of male animus projective energy, is the full concept of receptive anima femininity, I'm starting with what is always going to be good and right about me. What I'm also saying is that my experience, my childhood dynamics, became like a transparency or an overlay that went over my eyes—eyes meaning e-y-e, therefore it colored my perception and I, which also means how I see myself. When I focus on the imprint of how I was created, I can push away, I can dissolve these transparencies.

So I'm going to continue from a potential positive paradigm and not the negative, dysfunctional paradigm. So here we have the mother-father principle. We continue with the first stage of growth. Now these stages of growth are wide, and they are about emotional steps. They are merely to categorize certain experiences in our lives that we will have no matter what. The birth act, the action of when you were born, to begin with, is the first stage of your growth. The best example of how we are really born—not who in our family genetically had diabetes and the fact that it gets passed on to us, and who the alcoholic was and it got passed on to us, and who the musician or the artist was and that got passed on to us, that's a biological imprint—from a spiritual, energetic, attitudinal imprint, comes from a book called *An Outline of Spiritual Healing* by Gordon Turner.[49] He says that at the moment in which you're born, you are absolutely at the height of evolution. He explains that if you

---

[49]   Gordon Turner, *An Outline of Spiritual Healing* (New York: Warner Paperback Library, 1972).

follow through the pregnancy, what actually is repeated is all of evolution, from a one-cell principle to an amphibian stage to the first vertebrate, and then so forth to the nervous system and finally to human. According to him this is a spiritual reminder that you carry with you in your DNA the full, total memory of all life. At the very moment you are born, you are the sum total of all evolution at that moment, and if a baby were born a minute later, that baby is the sum total, and so on. And so we do have all memory in an inner conscious, or collective unconscious, imprint in us, in this spiritual, energetic way, and so what we're carrying is not just the history of our own mother and father, but the history of life.

Now, return to this positive paradigm that says I lead; the minute I'm born I'm born a leader because all of evolution is behind me, and I am born with the full power of God and carrying a torch that says because I am alive and because I have freedom to choose I can make a difference—now, watch this—for all generations past and all generations forward. Why? Because energy is dynamic. It cannot be destroyed or created, only transformed. Your energy in the moment moves in all directions, both to the past and into the future. When I change my attitude, my mind, through prayer, meditation, affirmation, I literally change in the moment the point of power in the present, but that moves backwards in time as well as forward in time. I transcend time when I truly grow from the spiritual sense. This is who you were born to be. You were born to be the transcendent peacemaker. It is by the nature and definition of energy that we have this ability, and so again I can't just go back one generation to my mother and father and say, "Here I am in the present, 2002, stuck." I'd be insulting my own intelligence. I'd be insulting your intelligence. I'd be insulting the power of God within you that is beyond all time and space.

So when I rise above, I am out of the trappings of *chronos* time, which is linear and day by day, and I evolve into *cairos* time, which is a spiral time that says, "In a single moment." In *A Course in Miracles* it

169

is called the *holy instant.*[50] The holy instant is the moment I recognize that the eternity of God is within me and that when I change my mind and see the past as separate from me, not having power over me because of the power within me, I am released from its bondage, from its fear, from its sickness and disease, from its entrapments, from its limitations, and in that moment I free up the future to be as I see it: healthy, happy, peaceful, and prosperous. I can change my family history by changing myself. What they do with the information may only affect them on a spiritual and mental plane and I may not see the difference physically, but the energy went to them and they too were given the chance to change. If they choose it, so be it; if they don't, so be it. But my responsibility, my exercising of my inherited birthright, is to change me, not anybody else. You can't change somebody, whether it is your mother or your father or your brother or your sister or your son or daughter. You cannot change them; you only change yourself. Most of the time, when we are trying to change somebody else it is an ego convenience, because it would serve us in the moment if they would grow in a way that we want them to grow. Most of the time, when we want somebody else to change, it's because we in fact will not change. We have chosen not to change. And so, from birth you have been given this power of eternity to change and transcend time by you releasing yourself from the entrapments of the past.

Let's move into the next stage of life, up to about three or four years old. What happens overall? These are wide categories that only serve the purpose of showing some emotional changes and how we can get out of them. Most of the time, we spend our lives repeating emotional behaviors and trying to change the behavior, not connecting and understanding that we must change our minds before we change our behaviors. We must change what we think and feel before we can change what we do. What happens between

---

50   Foundation for Inner Peace, *A Course in Miracles* (Farmingdale, NY: Coleman, 1975), 1:280.

the ages of about two and four is that we become language literate. We think, we speak, we converse. This act of voice is the first act of creation. The very first few verses of Genesis say: "And God said let there be light and there was light." It was the word that created the deed. We have this power given to us before the age of three that as you say it, so you become. "As a man thinketh in his heart, so he is." So that means that even the words that you say to yourself as well as to others, the words that you have absorbed from others, are making a reality. From this healthy, transcendent, spiritual paradigm, at any moment in time I can correct any preconceived, stamped notion that language might have stamped onto me because of what I heard, because of what I said. Again, I can transcend time.

At two and three and four, the typical thing that we heard was the word *no*. You heard, "No." You heard, "Bad boy, bad girl; good boy, good girl." You heard, "Ask your mother; ask your father." I heard that a lot. You heard, "You can't; you're not allowed; you don't have permission to; you're too little." And overall, whether you had good or bad parents is not the issue. It's that the imprint of that language taught you that your word doesn't count. No matter how old you are now, you can transcend time. The point of power is in the present. You can stand right where you are, right here, right now, and vow out of your birthright to simply do one thing and you will erase all of that, and that is to keep your word, to simply say what you mean and mean what you say. Trust me, this is no easy task. If you did everything that you said you were going to do, in some cases you'd become rich and famous overnight, while in other cases you would be arrested.

The point about language is that the first act of creation, God saying, "Let there be light and there was light," was given to you. What is it that you say, and are you willing to reclaim the birthright that was given to you between two and three and four years old and keep your word? Keep your word, say what you mean and mean what you say, and you will eliminate 60 percent of your problems.

Most of people's problems, whether they are attitudinal or physical, are because they have talked themselves into it. We have, at this point, talked ourselves right into the condition that we are calling our personal reality, and I say then talk yourself out of it. But it won't stick, it won't change, if you only pay lip service to it. Where you've got to do the self-talk is where it counts, where the power lives. The power doesn't live on the language of the lips. The power lives in the language of the soul, in your gut, in prayer, in humility, in silence, where you vow to your mother God or father God, "I will change my language." Unless you are willing to change your words, you are not willing to change. In this, you will begin the process of learning the father principle and the mother principle by merely watching your language and keeping your word.

The next stage of growth is between three and six. Again, these are wide, emotional categories, and I'm using a whole different system than what we have seen and read in books like *Educational Psychology* from Erik Erikson and *Stages of Growth and Development* by Abraham Maslow. These are different. In fact, I will call them *Gingerized*, which means I created them. Between three and six what we notice is differences: who's tall, who's short; who's thin, who's fat; who's dark, who's white; who's green-eyed, blue-eyed; who's got curly hair and who's got straight hair; who has big hands, a big nose, big lips; who sings; who dances; who walks funny. We notice the differences. We see that we are different. This is the first step in becoming an individual—what we have the ability to do innately and can again transcend all time. Even if you didn't learn it between the ages of three and six, you can do it now, you can do it today.

You are as different as there are no two snowflakes alike. Now, isn't it ironic that this ability gives birth to itself out of you, out of the power of God, somewhere between three and six years old? Of course, the four-year-old, the five-year-old, or the six-year-old does not have the intellectual capacity to recognize his or her own individuality, but the seed was planted, and you can transcend all the pain you might have endured because you thought in those early years, whether they were grammar school or high school, that being different was in fact wrong. You can transcend that because right now you can look around and you can see there are no two roses that are the same, no two sunsets, no two sunrises. Go to the beach. You want to talk about differences? Go to the beach and see how many differences. Go to the mall and sit and watch. You want to understand that your God is a God of variety? Go to the mall and have a religious experience, and see that no two people are going to walk the same, talk the same. People are going to look at a display window and some people are going to go, "Ooh la la, Sassoon," and somebody else is going to say, "Oh, look at that. Isn't that ridiculous?" Your God is a God of variety and you were born different because different means individual. You're not supposed to be like anybody else. So the seed of this was planted in you potentially between the ages of three and six.

What we did was to create a neurosis out of it. We tried all of our lives to fit in while we're feeling different and left out. We tried to comb our hair the same, walk the same, dress the same, or do the complete opposite: "I'm not doing it that way. I'm doing this. I'm shaving my head." And if there is one thing that you do not have to fight for, because it is God ordained, it is your individuality. The imprint of who you are in your soul, your personality, is so unique you will never be duplicated again, and for some of you, your friends are saying right now, "Thank God." But who knew that this was the seed?

And so, now in adulthood what can we do? In adulthood, right now, in the moment, in the present, you can transcend all time and reclaim your individuality, and know that the way that you think, the way that you feel, the way that you love is simply coming out of your individuality, and the only criterion about individuality is that it must be rooted in peace and truth. If what you are expressing to the external world is anything less than peaceful and truthful, you have reduced yourself to being less than human. You are not functioning as a human being. You have dropped down a notch on the evolutionary scale. As far as I know, what is beneath human is animal. When I am rooted in peace and truth is the only way, the only time that I will fully be me, that there will be no doubt about my individuality. There will be no second-guessing it. There will be no lack of confidence and absolutely, as sure as the heavens and the earth, there will be no doubt about who I am as a person. I will accept me for the first time, and guess what? What I send out is what comes back. When I accept me, so will the rest of the world. People treat you the way that you teach them to treat you, for better or worse. Self-criticism will breed attack. Self-judgment will breed emotional violence in all relationships. All of this was given to you in the seedlings between three and six years old, and you can reclaim it by going within and releasing it in prayer; in peace and truth know who you are.

The next phase—and believe it or not, it's the last one—happens at about seven or eight. What happens then? It is called the *age of reason*, and we are given at that age, seven or eight, the potential, like a bud that didn't open, the ability from God—not your parents, from God—to think and choose, fear or love. The age of reason is about choosing what is morally right, what is honest, based on what is loving or fearful. Now, who at seven years old is capable of doing that? With all the Velcro, you're lucky the seven-year-old can tie his shoes. But you again can transcend time, right now, and reclaim that gift that God gave you at seven or eight, and know in prayer, in quiet and silent prayer with God, choosing is your birthright, love over fear. At this point, the whole of the human race can change.

What is it that I am saying? That all of the imprints to be God-like, to be made in the image and likeness of God, are truly given by age seven? Yes, I am. What else am I saying? I am saying that all of us stopped growing at age six. That's what I'm saying, and we constantly choose fear instead of love. We are so riveted to fear that we think unless we have something to be afraid of, there's something to be afraid of. We don't even know what it looks like to live a peaceful life. We don't even know what it looks like to be in love a lot—six months, then we'll talk. We don't know what it is to be happy, healthy, and prosperous.

If we follow this model of how I really think that we were born, I believe you and I together, the micro—the tiny dot, as tiny as an atom—can put the earth back on its axis, because we will choose love over fear; we will reclaim, transcend time; we will make proper choices; we will keep our word; we will reclaim that the mother-father God is within at all times, always protecting, always guiding; and then you and I will begin to live heaven on earth, now. Now! We will begin to be the peacemakers of the world. This is our destiny. Our only reason to be alive on this planet now, regardless of how many years we will live (and we can change that, too; we can change the quality of today, promise ourselves a better quality tomorrow) is that we must become peacemakers and the peace starts with us. We will never make peace with our families. We will never make peace with warring nations and countries. We will never make peace with all races, creeds, religions, all sexual preferences. We will never make peace unless we make peace with ourselves and know that we are good because God said so, and that nobody else's opinion—including our own—counts. We will limit ourselves first and the rest of the world will simply imitate us. "Blessed are the peacemakers." What follows that? "For they shall inherit the earth." You and I, for the first time, will inherit the kingdom, but we must first make peace in the micro and then in every day truly look to every single human being as our mother, our father, our brother, our sister, our son, or our daughter.

Choose love over fear and keep your word. This is enough for any twenty-four-hour day. Have milk and cookies and go to bed. Wake up tomorrow and start again. To me, this is the key to the kingdom. We have enough information right now. Act on it and make peace.

Your Worksheet B

We're going to do another exercise to teach you how to make peace in your whole family and then how to begin to live this in your everyday life.

- Allow yourself to be comfortable, feet flat on the floor, or in the most relaxed position that you can be in. If you have glasses, remove them. For those of you who wear contacts, when you're at home it could probably help you to take them off, also, just so that you can make a little difference in your vision when you open your eyes. It has an effect of actually changing your perception of things, because there's such an energy bath when you do meditate in this manner that when you open your eyes, it's kind of like the metaphor of you seeing differently, both from *e-y-e* and the pronoun *I*.
- So begin now with your eyes closed, and begin to breathe in and breathe out and take your time, breathing in and breathing out and relaxing. It is good in fact to even repeat the word *relax* as you continue to breathe in and out, in and out. Let each breath become a little deeper and a little slower. Let each breath now become the golden light, as if you were made of sunlight. Breathing in every cell of your body is this golden light. The light is strength; the light is wisdom; the light is the peace of God. Relax.
- At the count of three, you'll again imagine yourself in that beautiful garden, in some open-air, natural setting where you feel the most peaceful. One, two, three. Let all of nature be represented—sense it, feel it, smell it, and really allow yourself to be there. Notice again how nature has a harmonious vibration and flow through it. Relax and go deeper. Allow yourself to imagine that you're having a picnic. Some of your favorite foods are there. You're just enjoying yourself, and you

can even see the sunshine pouring through the very cells, the very pores of your skin. You feel radiant. You feel alive and vibrant. You feel holy and at peace.

- At the count of three, you're going to have a picture image of you at birth. One, two, three. Sense you as a newborn infant and see yourself the way God did, perfect, radiant, and that inscribed on your soul is God's own signature of goodness, of power, and that all your life you would, day by day, have an opportunity to release this power, this strength, and to become more fully you. See that newborn, beautiful and talented and radiant, and then imagine that you literally pick this infant up and press this infant in a hug into your chest and the baby becomes light and enters back into your body, this being a metaphor of you reclaiming from birth the true you, as a child of God, as you were created.

- Now, at the count of three, you will imagine yourself to be two or three or four years old. One, two, three. And see yourself able to speak, to talk, to listen, to converse, remembering the beautiful expression of truth, "Out of the mouths of babes truth is spoken." You'll look at yourself at two and three and four, and you see yourself as a little one, a child of grace, now able to speak your true self; you will speak the truth—you will keep your word. You have released this power that God has given you way back at two or three or four years old, and you see this beautiful child now, able to speak and create a personal reality that is happy and healthy and prosperous, and let this child of two or three run to your arms and embrace this child, and let the child become pure energy and enter back into your body. You now are using what God gave you, knowledge and language, and you keep your word.

- Relax and continue now. At the count of three, you'll see yourself somewhere between three, four, five, six years old, school age. One, two, three. See yourself off to school, carrying books, being with other children, and for the first time seeing how you are different. But you see yourself as an individual and different. In fact, you see everybody as individual and different. You are not less than; you are not victimized for being different because of shape, because of color, because of where you came from, because of your religion, because of your own unique way of being. In fact, what you do is you see all the other kids as reflections of God, and you come to understand how good God is, that the Creator sees fit to make a variety of images that he calls all the children of the world, and you peel off all false prejudices, all hidden false prejudices that others have placed on you. You reclaim your individuality because God gave it to you, and now this little school child of five or six runs to you and you embrace the child, and you take back the true self. You feel good to be the individual. It is good to be who you are. And that child turns into energy and you take back your individuality, and you are finally free.

• Relax, and now at the count of three you'll see yourself as seven or eight. One, two, three. Now you know the difference. Now you have power of language. Now you know there is a mother-father God within you, and so you can walk the earth, conscious, alert, and aware, ready to choose love over fear, regardless of the situation, how great and how small. This is what is in the seven—or eight-year-old, and you will reclaim that now. You will bring it back home inside yourself, and so now this little person knows what love is and has felt it from within, has felt it from the mother-father God from within. This little person has felt it by the act of creation that language gives us from within, and has felt it by the individuality of being unique and different from within, and you choose love, and you choose love, and you choose love. And so the eight-year-old, this little person unique and complete, rushes to you, and you embrace your own self, and you now as the eight-year-old turn into energy and you melt back inside as pure energy, and you say, "I am the peace of God in all things great and small. I am the peace of God." That is, *p-e-a-c-e* and *p-i-e-c-e*. This is the truth, so be it. This is who you are in true growth and development, so be it. Amen.

• Relax. When you are comfortable to do so, open your eyes. Take a few moments in quiet to reflect on your own experiences and emotional responses or ideas or images.

To continue to carry this experience with you, it is good to repeat any stage, any phase, from birth to two and three years, from three to six years old, and from seven or eight years old. And to recapture the whole significance, it is good to simply repeat to yourself, "I am the peace of God," and see it in your mind spelled *p-e-a-c-e* as well as *p-i-e-c-e*. When you know that you are that peace of God and that no one—no man, no woman, no dog, no cat, no canary—can ever take that away from you, you'll become the peacemaker of the world and you will inherit the kingdom. Amen.

Chapter Nine

One Love, One Law, One Life

What Happened to Me

It was the summer of '87. My dear friend and priest, Father Albert, was dying of an aggressive lymphoma. He was diagnosed in April and by July 27, 1987, he would become an angel.

Our visits were intense in those days. Time didn't matter. I wanted so much to change what was inevitable. My friend was dying. I was so caught between my desires and his needs. In my heart, all I could pray at the time was, "Please don't die."

In the ending days, the silence together became poignant. I watched him peacefully accept to yield to God even through all the pain in his body. "Just be happy in your heart," he would say. "Remember, God is Real. Love is Real. Don't be afraid. There is no time or space that is without God's Love. His Love is everywhere."

Something happened when I heard those words. He was dying, but the lessons of love were not.

I still cry sometimes. Father Albert was such an important influence for so many people. I would think, "What if I never met him?" He taught me to feel God inside, not just know about God.

There are no accidents. The life we live is all about loving and learning to love more. The law is simple. Whoever is in front of you is related to you. Be kind, be respectful, be happy. God loves all His children equally.

How You See It

Whenever somebody talks about love, he or she can have diametrically opposed views, which is usually, "This was the one love of my life," and there's usually a tragedy after that—you know, second to none less than Romeo and Juliet, or Maria and Tony.

The other side of that polarity is that true love never happens, like in one of my favorite movies, *Lovers and Other Strangers*,[51] a great movie in which all kinds of relationships are represented. Bea Arthur plays the mother, an Italian mother, and Richard Castellano plays the Italian father, and the whole story revolves around their two sons. The one son is getting a divorce, and they're not able to bring this up to the family because, you know, "We don't divorce in my family. No divorce—stay together for the sake of the kids." Like they know what's going on anyway. And the other son is living with his girlfriend, so he says he's living with a roommate, whatever his name is. Now, today it would be completely reversed, and they would rather his roommate were his girlfriend and fiancée, so certainly times have changed. But the whole thing was about the sign of the times in terms of what makes for a relationship, and it revolved around this festive, gala wedding. One of my favorite lines in the movie is when Bea Arthur finally finds out that Richie, her son, is getting a divorce, while they're sitting in the living room with plastic seat covers (because nobody goes in there) and plastic fruit in a plastic bowl. She sits, and she says to her son, "What's wrong? What do you mean? I don't understand this, that you're getting a divorce, it's not working. What's not working? How could it not work? What is the problem in this? What are you looking for? Are you looking for

---

[51] *Lovers and Other Strangers*, Twentieth Century-Fox Company, 1971.

happiness? Don't look for happiness—it'll only make you miserable." There's something very cynical about this.

We write poetic verses and we sing love songs in our own minds and in our own ways, and there's a dying swan in our lives someplace, and we can't talk about love and relationships without addressing whether there is such a thing as the "love of my life." I mean, do you love once? Is there this perfect fit, hand-in-glove? You know, "We connected." Now that's the terminology. That's a millennium thing: "We just connected; we bonded." In the sixties and seventies, we were talking about the same kind of special love, but the term was, "We have vibrations. We have the same vibratory channel." Maybe now that we're in the twenty-first century, it will be something like, "Well, we had our auras checked and it's a perfect match." But in any way that we're describing it, we always seem to be looking for a perfect partner.

And we always go out with those two extremes. We either had it and lost it, it died, it went away, he was married, or the other side is, "Don't look for that. Go for the security, check his bank account, and deal with it from there." I heard a not-so-young comedienne who said, "You know, I'd like to find an older man—you know, somewhat older than me. I just think I could relate to it better." And then she said, "You know, somebody who's really kind and generous, and somebody with a big heart." Her timing was explicit in this, and she concluded, "Even an enlarged heart would be good, with a couple of valves that are dysfunctional—that would even be better."

I have a friend for whom every love of her life is the true love of her life, and not to make a joke of the tragedy, but three times these supposed love-of-her-life men literally died, so the joke with us was, "They're dying to love you."

So the question still is: Is there such a thing as this perfect love, this perfect relationship, this perfect partner? Again, before we can answer that question, we have to understand the nature of love, the natural substance of love, and the natural substance of love is not human but divine. Is there a perfect partner? Yes, there is. The answer is yes. It is the source within you, which doesn't mean that you should go home and hug your novena books. It means we have to understand the substance of love so that the form of love, which is called relationship, can be much more approachable, available, and also reliable in our lives.

In the last eighty years at least on this planet, we have separated the head from the heart in matters of life and love. We have become such a robotlike society in this age of mechanization, in this age of materialism, that we have literally intellectualized everything. We have put all aspects of our lives in these neat little Ziploc bags and separated them. We see this in terms of health care. Even in terms of education we see this. Years ago, education took place in a one-room schoolhouse, certainly not to say that that was the best, and then it evolved and we started to fragment our educational process into five class periods a day, five subjects, etc. Soon kids did not understand the connection between the historical times and the art of that historical time, nor did they connect the literature as it influenced the art of that period. Everything simply got fragmented, and this fragmentation of life is the long-term result of the industrial revolution on how we live and love.

We did this in medicine. We have specialists for literally everything, where years ago you had a general practitioner who took care of you and your whole family and was just a step up from a farm doctor, but knew a whole case history and integrated the emotional components with the physiological components, and knew the stress of your life and how it would affect your relationships and how it would affect your body.

Technology advanced, and in order for us to try to keep up we cut everything into little pieces to try to digest it, understand it, and in some cases, control it. We did this in our personal lives. We put people in categories. This is my friend in business and this is my favorite cousin, this is my special love interest and this is just whom

I sleep with. We really did fragment all of this, as if there were different kinds of love.

What It Really Is

There is only one love. There is only one law to that love and there is only one life to live in love following the one law, and before we can understand how we can let this one love, one law, and one life move through us and express itself out into the world, we have to get clear once again about the nature of love. Love is the source of light that is called God breathing within you. What we do with the love is human. The expression of the love is human. The essence of the love is divine. Because of that, we can't define it exclusively. We'll never get to define totally what love is. It doesn't, however, stop us from expressing it, being it, interacting with it, much like we can't really define electricity. It's very difficult to define electricity, but it doesn't stop any of us from entering into a dark room and finding the light switch. We look for the light switch and turn it on, not really knowing how it works. In fact, when, nearly fifty years ago, they split the atom and wanted to find out what really was in there—what was the tiniest particle of energy of life—they couldn't. They said it was the invisible energy between the electrons, protons, neutrons; it's in there. It was the space between, like the hole in a doughnut.

Deepak Chopra[52] also talks about the power breath of life as the space between the thoughts and the breath that you take in the thoughts. How can you hold onto that single moment and capture it and identify it and put it in a bottle, in a jar, and then try to duplicate it? You can't, and this is part of our problem in identifying real love and expressing real love.

---

[52] Deepak Chopra, M.D., *Ageless Body, Timeless Mind* (New York: Harmony Books, 1993), 264-267.

On top of this, we have all been victimized by the fragmentation of society as a result of the overindustrialization of our culture, of our society. An example of this is how you and I probably came to know about God. How you came to learn about God was probably through a cerebral, intellectual experience. You were taught rules and regulations. If you were raised in a Catholic Christian background, you probably studied from the *Baltimore Catechism* or from the Bible. If you were raised in the Hebrew tradition, you learned from the Torah. You learned from some scriptural accounts. They were to be studied. They were to be perceived and learned and understood through the mind.

Here's the problem. The language of God is felt in the soul. As long as we keep trying to understand God through the mind, we are always going to perceive that power called the Creator, called the Author of Life, through our perceptions. So if we have a problem with our own father, have a problem with our own mother, it's pretty likely that we're going to project that onto God. Freud even says that a lot of extremely religious people are nearly fanatical based on some carryover projection transfer due to parental experiences.[53] We learned about God as some set of rules to follow—to get it right, to be perfect.

What I have noticed in my own experience, being in this kind of educational transformation business now for over twenty-five years, is that the void in people's lives—the biggest void in people's lives—is always about love. The hurt is always about love. Somehow love hurt them.[54] It was through a father, a mother, a brother, a sister, a son or daughter, a spouse, a lover, but there was damage. There was a tear in the heart somehow, and from that they lost hope in their lives, and

---

[53] Sigmund Freud, *The Future of an Illusion*, trans. and ed. by James Strachey (New York: W. W. Norton, 1961), 17-19.

[54] M. Scott Peck, M.D., *The Road Less Traveled* (New York: Simon and Schuster, 1978), 15-18.

they lost the ability to have the vision that they could literally live happy, healthy, and prosperous lives. I have found that that void, that hole, that hurt, that tear in the heart does not originate from the pain that was transferred in a personal relationship with another human being, but in fact is a void from not having a personal experience with God.

You may be somebody who has already had a personal experience with God. If you are, you know that it is not an intellectual experience. It's something that you feel way down deep inside of you. The Greek word is *splachna*,[55] meaning "the seat of the soul," where we would know way down in the gut, in the belly. In Hindu it would be the spleen, *chockra*, where this happens. When you pray deeply and intensely, you are without words, you are without mind, you are soulful, and from that *splachna*, the womb of who you are, you come to know God through a feeling of the presence that is awesome.

We associate the word *awe* with the word *fear*, even though it did not originate from the word fear. It originated from exactly the expression that happened when early people had spiritual experiences, way back thousands of years ago. Moses speaks of it. The Rabbi Jesus speaks of it. Other avatars speak of when they had the experience of God. It's also discussed by William James.[56] The only thing you do is you have an expression with your breath, with your breathing, "Aaaaah," and the sound you make sounds like the word *awe*. You take a breath in, and you are overwhelmed by the beauty and the presence that is within you, and you come then to recognize that this is God.

The power of that personal experience with God is that you are transformed. You are never, ever the same again, because in that

---

[55] *Splagkhna*—Greek for intestines. Compassion is intestinal. Tender mercy is possibly translated as *diasplagkhna ilious*.

[56] William James, *The Varieties of Religious Experience* (New York: Macmillan, 1961), 60-68.

single moment you absolutely are certain, without a shadow of a doubt, that God knows you by name and loves you. In fact, I will say is in love with you. Nothing in our society enables us to have that kind of experience; not even our religious organizations really make room for feeling the presence of God. It is done more through a left brain, rather than a right brain, cerebral experience, yet mystics, the contemplatives—such people as Teresa of Avila, John of the Cross in the Christian world, the prophets of the Old Testament—were certainly not PhDs. They were not doctors of divinity. They were shepherds. If they could read and write, good for them, but that is not what made them prophets. It was the gnawing in their bellies that said, "I cannot ignore this feeling," and they gave in to it. Every one of the early prophets had these very intuitive, mystical, right brain—as we would call them now—experiences about God, and if you read through the Old Testament, it's rich in love. It's rich in a love story about how they tried to resist; they tried to resist this feeling that was inside of them because they felt they were not the ones to be responsible for carrying out the message. I even think that the story about Jonah floundering in the belly of the whale is about us struggling with our own bellies, the feeling that gets us in the gut whenever we allow love to begin to happen.

The problem is without a personal experience of God, we are not aware of what true love feels like, so we try to think it through some kind of logical something or other, and that is going to end up keeping us in these Ziploc bags of what will keep us secure. Prophets in the Old Testament (Dan. 10:15-19) took their fear with them and surrendered because of some gut intuition that said, "I must answer this." Even Gibran, in the book *The Prophet*,[57] says, "When you love you yield to the presence that is within you," which is that same mentality, that same real holistic mentality, about how to get close to God. Daniel is a young prophet who is absolutely

---

[57] Kahlil Gibran, *The Prophet* (New York: Alfred A. Knopf, 1923), 12.

certain that he is too young to be a prophet. Abraham is absolutely certain that he is too old to be the one that God would choose. His wife, absolutely certain that she's barren and past her years to give Abraham a child, wonders how she could follow God's plan and considers herself cursed. The Apostles of the New Testament were to me the best example of misfits and flunkies. You had a tax collector and you had Paul, later on in the Acts of the Apostles (Acts, 2 Cor. 6:14-19), who was literally a hitman who persecuted Christians. God chooses the "everyman" and the "everywoman," you and me, and that gnawing in the belly is the invitation to come home to the one love of your life, to live the one law in your life, so that all your life will be loving and safe.

We are those people of the Old and New Testaments. We are the prophets who struggled in the Torah. We are the frightened Apostles and new disciples of the Acts of the Apostles after the death and story of resurrection from the Rabbi Jesus. We are those frightened children, because we're trying to figure something out from fragmented beings. We're trying to drink of the waters of God through our heads. We're trying to absorb this power and this presence through reading a book, through studying, and what I have found is that this may cultivate the soil, but the only place to learn about love is to learn about it from the love giver, from the originator of love, and that is the one within you. There is no one who will love you more than your Creator. There is no one who will care for you, about you, provide for you, all your life. There is no essence, no ability greater than the power of God within you. In fact, we have throughout time given three adjectives to this presence of God: *omnipotent*, meaning all-powerful; *omniscient*, meaning all-knowing; and *omnipresent*, meaning everywhere, and this is the power of God that is within you.

It is awesome to think that tiny little you and tiny little me are made of the same substance that truly created the entire universe, and throughout the last century we have pulled away from the light and moved closer to machines and technologies and gadgets and all kinds of things that will dazzle us with their supposed power. The technological advances will make our lives absolutely convenient. They will make a network around the globe. They will help us to connect brother to sister and mother to father and to child, all around the globe. But before the full impact of that happens we have got to know the source or we will pay homage to false gods, and that is what we have done in our relationships; so we need a picture.

It's very difficult to comprehend the power of God. It always has been and it always will be, and the way to come that I have found to be really close to that love, the first true intimate example, intimate relationship that you will ever have in your life is in silence. Isaiah says, "Be still and know that I am your God." In the silence, we shut down the chatter of perception and the educated brain and we let the *splachna*, the womb within us, the core of our existence, speak on its own. What we have erroneously tried to do is to go out into the world and let other people teach us about love when the only teacher of love is God. Our first lover must be the one within us. Without that, how will I know what love is? I have to be able to get deep enough in me to feel the presence, feel it, let it so permeate me physically as well as mentally and spiritually that the existence of God, the truth about God, the peace about God, will never be a question in my mind again. I will have questions. I will have problems. I will have challenges. I will be sad, mad, happy, and glad all in a single day, but it will have nothing to do with me questioning the source of my life.

When I allow enough time on a regular daily basis—that's why I believe it is "Give us thy daily bread," come to me daily and feed me, Lord, from within—I then can feel what that love feels like and then translate that through imitation, meaning I will mimic that as I interact with you. My job is to feel the way I feel inside, to pay attention to that feeling, and then duplicate it with others. That is the true message of the only two laws that there ever are in life: that you should love your God with your whole heart, mind, body, and soul, completely. That is the first cause, to love your God. How could I love you if I do not know who the source of me is, if I do not know what the Author of Love is? And the second law is merely the expression of the first: that you should love your neighbor as yourself. I can't love you until I love me. I can't love me until I know that I am lovable. The one who is going to show me my true value and lovability is not another person, because he or she will fall short by perception, but God. To know that my value comes from within and is unshakable, I then begin to live a new life, a totally new life.

Through prayer, silence, and meditation you will come to know the two main aspects of yourself, and that is that you are both invincible and you are vulnerable. You are invincible from within. Nothing, no matter what, how great or how small, can ever have power over your life, because the spirit of you, the essence of you, the core of you is invincible, and in your humanness you are vulnerable. I choose to stay vulnerable because it will help me to relate to the pain of the planet and to feel the suffering of others and then, out of my invincibility, I can draw upon that like an endless well of healing waters, and reach out in a better way to serve, to help, to be a healing agent. Yes, we could hurt each other for a while. You could hurt my feelings, but you cannot hurt my life. You can hurt my body; you cannot hurt my life. And we have to have a different image to help us get to the source, or we will continue to blame others and say, "There goes the love of my life. He's going to the mall with his wife."

So let's make another picture to help us to see both this invincibility and vulnerability that truly is the one love and one law, one life, that we are to live. For me, I picture it as sunshine, because it's available and it has some science to it that I can really relate to. So let's picture a high noon sun and it's a perfect, clear day. Extended from the sun are the sun's rays. Each ray is made of the same particles as the sun. Whatever a ray of the sun can do, so too does the full essence, the full sphere of the sun, but certainly a ray of the sun is not equal to the full capacity of the sun. I can't break a ray of the sun away from the source of the sun. They are eternally connected. In fact, to try to break it is insane. That is the relationship you have with God. The source, the full dynamics of the sun is God, and you and I are rays—individualistic, extending, and rooted from the source but extending out of it, doing all the same things, capable of doing all the same things as this full sunlight, but certainly not equal to it. What we do in love is we recognize that each one of us is connected to the same lover, the same source, the same light, and as that same power essence pours through you, it is expressed differently. It still carries with it peace and truth when it is truly God-like, and it will have with it a dressing of your individual personality, and so it is God, the essence, moving through Holly, allowing Holly to be more Holly. It is God the source moving through Sandy, allowing Sandy to be more of who she is. It is God the source moving through Michael, allowing Michael to become more of Michael.

And what happens is when we meet, what we are seeing through each other is a specific expression of love. It's like having a point of view. The point of view is only one point to see a whole view: the full view of the sun, 360 degrees. The more we allow ourselves to see how the other person loves and expresses, the more we will get closer to understanding a 360-degree view. The difference between the way that you love and the way that God loves is that your love is a point of view, a ray of that love, and the power of God is the whole view. That's why it is called *universe*, one turn equaling 360 degrees, and not *unisquare*. So the more that we allow the love to come through us, extending it, the more it comes back. That's the law. It's one love moving through you. You let it out. It is personalized by who you are in your person. The more love comes back. That's the one law. And the one life is that we are sharing in God's life, God's breath of life. So is there one true love? Yes, and it is the source within you, and each person whom you encounter is to help you to free up and love God more, and in that you will be able to love yourself because you'll feel your value. You'll feel your significance. There is no way people can feel important in this life if they haven't surrendered to God and found out through a feeling that they are loved, that they are deeply loved.

The first lines in *A Course in Miracles* say: "Nothing real can be threatened. Nothing unreal exists. Herein lies the peace of God."[58] That describes the combination of the invincibility that you are because of God's essence and love in you and the vulnerability. "Nothing real can be threatened." The real you is that you're always and forever connected to God. You cannot separate away. "Nothing unreal exists." What does this mean? Your own opinion of you doesn't count. What blocks us from our ability to let God really be this prime mover in our lives, prime lover, prime intimate love affair as the example, is guilt, because somewhere in our lives we do innately know—much like we innately have the archetypes of good and evil and justice and authority and mother and father within us—that we didn't create ourselves. We know the source is God, and our guilt is that we chose someone, some person, some thing, some place, some substance, and made it into our God, and this guilt is what keeps us from going deep enough in silence. We already know the one love. We already know the one law. We know innately that it's one life, but it is the guilt that separates us.

We have to be able to reclaim the feeling, because if we go through these intellectual steps all over again about how to figure out who God is, we'll only get caught in what one friend called *transformed clutter*. We'll get stuck and trip over one neurotic day after another. We'll one day figure out that we're okay and the next day we're not, and the one day it's her fault, the next day it's his fault, and the next day it's my fault, and there still is a blame game going on.

Is there a perfect love? Yes, you are breathing it. You are breathing it, but are you allowing it to touch you? We are very out of touch with

---

58   Foundation for Inner Peace, Introduction to *A Course in Miracles* (Farmingdale, NY: Coleman, 1975).

one another. We're afraid to touch. We're afraid to hug. We're afraid to shake hands. We're afraid to embrace. You must have a relative in your family who is the worst hugger that God ever put breath in. I have one aunt who puts her makeup on with a spatula, and when you go to hug her you get this hard corner of a cheekbone because you shouldn't mess up her face: "Oh, my face. Watch my hair, my face." And then there are other people who, when they go to shake your hand, you think all their fingers had been broken just prior to that handshake.

So I believe that the void in our lives is that we're looking for the one true love, but much like the song, we're looking for love in all the wrong places, and what we really have to do is go back home, inside, and just let God be the teacher of love. We falsify that by thinking and expecting that once there's a chemistry and attraction—"I like you." "Me, too"—that this person now is going to teach you about love. He or she can't; only God can.

It's very important to hear these initial words. No matter how many times I read the introductory words of *A Course in Miracles*, they mean more and clarify and peel off my vulnerability and make more evidence to my invincibility. They say this is "a course in miracles," *course* meaning a path, a way in miracles. To me, the word *miracle* means "little image." That's me, a little image. A little image of what? Of God. I am a reflection of him. The introduction says it is a required course. It says we must do this in this lifetime, only the time you take is voluntary, which says to me I could, in a single instant, have an opening, an awareness, a heightened experience, and I can grow a lifetime in a week or wait until my body is racked with a disease and I'm on my deathbed and I'm hooked up to machines and I have a moment of truth. I choose the first.

It continues, "Free will doesn't mean you establish the curriculum." *Here's our biggest problem*: We get to choose by free will when we're going to learn about love, but not how. Why? Because we don't even know what it is, because it's God—they're equal. God = love.

They are equal, but it's not a banner. It's a presence that does feel. It then continues to say, "It means only"—referring to free will—"that you can elect what you want to take at a given time." Your free will is about whether you are going to accelerate your growth or procrastinate and delay it. You know this. You've seen this in people. We're great judges of others, saying, "Well, you know, if they would only do this, and if they would only do that—well, it would all work out," but when it comes to us, our favorite answer is, "Oh, I just don't know. I just don't know."

The introduction continues and says, "The course does not aim at teaching the meaning of love"—a very important statement, for that is beyond what can be taught. Why? Because God is the only teacher. God is the only healer. God will teach you who God is, and that power is love. Then it continues, "It does aim, however, at removing the blocks"—removing the vulnerability, removing the fear, removing the illusions, removing the insane perceptions that we have about ourselves and about others. It says, "It does aim, however, at removing the blocks to awareness of love's presence"—big ending—"which is your natural inheritance." The opposite of love is fear, but what is all-encompassing, love, can have no opposite. What is that saying? **Even fear doesn't exist—it's just the picture you make in your mind that makes it look like you'll fail, you'll lose, or you're not enough. That is your vulnerability, teaching you all you are is weak and vulnerable.** The deeper side of you, the true signature of who you are, is just that: deeper and invincible. That is God. And that's why "Nothing real can be threatened. Nothing unreal exists. Herein lies the peace of God."

So we must be able to have a better picture of the presence of God, and then come to know that that is the only source of who can teach you about what love is, what love feels like. The thing we do least in our busy, hectic, technologically correct lives is spend time inside ourselves and in silence. It is the thing that we need to do most. The key to your life is daily bread of a soulful ten or fifteen minutes a day, and to even keep a journal of just what it felt like—not judging it, but just responding to it. You feel good, you feel bad, you feel glad, you feel depressed, and know that always you have two sides—the invincible part of you, which is the love presence, and the vulnerable side of you, which is the fear's illusion, and then choose. That is the key to what I really believe life is. That is really what I believe we are meant to do.

I believe also that people will come into your life and trigger up a feeling, a deep, deep love feeling, that has no age. It can happen young, it can happen old, it can happen several times, it can happen in the most precarious of situations, but I believe that that person is an instrument to get you to feel in a world that says feelings are a sign of weakness. Be technologically and politically correct.

I believe that we are coming into a really important cycle in life, and I believe fifty years from now we may address it as the suffering years and then reevaluate it as the age of compassion. We have had more man-made and natural tragedies on the planet in the last generation, ten years, twenty years, with hurricanes and earthquakes and the threat of nuclear war where thousands, hundreds of thousands of people's lives have been in jeopardy for one reason or another. We have epidemic proportions of disease, like AIDS and cancer and heart disorders, and I believe that what is blatant in front of us is that the human being is suffering; but we keep trying to fix it from the outside in. What we need to do is first reach inside of ourselves and give God another chance.

If you search deep in your life, which is going to prepare us for this next exercise, you will come to understand that somewhere in your life the presence of God's love did come to you, did try to make you aware, but because God's presence, God's identity, is unconditional, it can't make you love back. It simply says, every breath you take, "I love you no matter what. Will you choose me?" That's what happens in every inhalation, in every exhalation, and somewhere in your life I believe God already came and started to open a door and started to try to get you to see the light within you, the part of you that is invincible, that is perfect and beautiful and has a purpose, and is unique and special and important to the rest of the planet, but you shut the door. You called it fear. "Uh, I'm afraid—afraid of the responsibility, afraid I can't trust the power, afraid that this isn't the truth," and I will say it was guilt that shut the door, guilt because somewhere else in your life you put a man, a woman, a child, a thing, a job, a substance, or money in place of that power and made it the source of your life, and in the guilt you then decided that God would punish you and cast you aside.

Look at the rays of the sun, how they are ever connected to the source of the sun, and know that that is your ongoing relationship with God that can never be separated under any circumstance, and come to know that even your guilt is human-made much like the fear, and what you have to do is be willing to go within again, in the silence, and find an experience in your life where the true presence of God started to touch you personally and you got scared. That's the point of this next exercise.

Your Worksheet A

- Allow yourself to be comfortable now, feet flat on the floor, or allow your body to be in a position that's comfortable, and take several deep breaths, with eyes closed. This time, as you breathe in and breathe out, really sense the feeling of golden light. Know that the feeling of the golden light within you is gentle and filled with wisdom and peace and comfort, and that every time you breathe in and breathe out, every cell of your body is releasing the invincible presence of God. Relax and go deeper.
- Feel the golden light as a soothing, deep peace. Feel the golden light as a soothing gentleness, as the open arms of your Creator, who waits for you every day to just come home

for a few moments in the day so that you could be fed your daily bread for the soul. Remain quiet now. Sense being in that beautiful, open meadow, that beautiful, open garden, where all of nature is represented. You see the beauty, you sense the harmony, and you really feel a oneness with the Creator. A gentleness, peace, and a strength totally fill you and somewhere deep inside, you hear, "I love you in all things great and small. I love you as I created you, carved you from the very palm of my hand, and this shall remain safe and with me always, even to the ends of the earth," says the Lord. And relax, and relax.

- Begin to feel that feeling, and at the count of three you will trust your very first impressions, and you will sense some experience in your life that you now can say was truly a time where there could have been an opportunity or an invitation to really get closer to God, but something stopped it and it frightened you. Always trust the first feeling, the first impression. One, two, three. Trust your gut, your intuition, your first instinct. What experience in your life, what loved person, what relationship, what problem was actually more about getting closer to God, and for what reason at that time did you stop it? Somewhere the fear and guilt stopped it and kept you feeling separated. Trust your first impression, what kept you from knowing the truth about the one that loves you most, the one that loves you best, God.

- Sometimes several experiences come to mind, opportunities to learn more about quiet time and prayer and listening, when you stopped because somewhere at that time a person, a job, a need, a substance was chosen as God. Somewhere you made a man, a woman, a career, money, a job, a substance abuse, food, sex, power, fame be the source as opposed to really let it be the true source that is God.

- Think of yourself as that ray of light connected to the sun. Know that you could never be separated, that it is an illusion, that it is an insane perception to think that God would turn his presence away from you or that you could turn your face away from that presence. What is equally as insane is the judgment that you placed upon yourself at that time. Let yourself be loved, first by God, and let that presence become the teacher so that all you do and say, think and feel will be rooted in this presence and you will draw more from the invincibility that you are than from the vulnerability. Relax.
- When you feel comfortable to do so, open your eyes and take a few moments to just reflect and respond to these ideas and feelings. A good affirmation to use is:

I choose to be rooted in the source of love within me so that all my expressions, all that I do, say, think, and feel are God-like.

When we spend a portion of the day in that silence, letting the teacher of love teach us about love, our whole perception of life changes. This is not an instant, overnight phenomenon. This is a steady progression of peeling layers and layers and layers of illusions from your perception. You can at any time accelerate it, and the key to the acceleration of the process is humility—and humility doesn't mean that you make yourself so less that you are beneath the lowest insect on the food chain. What it means is that you can clearly say to yourself, "Whatever it is that I have said about me or about life, including others and relationships, it is incomplete"—not wrong, because out of that you'll be making a judgment. You cannot love yourself while you remain in judgment. So to make yourself right or to make yourself wrong is a judgment.

The knowledge that we acquire in life will always be incomplete. The wisdom that we feel in the silence of prayer is what transcends all time and space and allows for the miracles to happen. The place of miracles is from that deep inside *splachna*, that deep inside holy, reverent feeling place, which we need actually a training to get to because we're so overstimulated in our culture. We suffer from a sensory bombardment. From the minute we get up, we have noise and distraction and noise and distraction—from television and radios, from traffic and people and sirens and horns, from shouting and talking, from garbage trucks and engines—and if we're going to move through this twenty-first century in a healthy, holistic, miraculous way, which I think we actually have the ability to do, we have to make a time and a place in our lives. Time means somewhere in your day, and place means a certain room, a chair, a porch, a church, a temple, a someplace that actually helps you to become silent. It doesn't have to be only one place. It can be several favorite spots—a walk in the woods, a stroll on the beach, a park—where you actually can tune out the noise and tune in to the silence, to the harmony that already exists.

We need to get closer to nature—to trees and leaves and grass and sand and oceans and mountains and rocks and streams—because the essence of God is in there too, and that's why when we have our vacation time and we seem to go more into these natural settings, we come back renewed. The spirit is rejuvenated because we have touched closer to heaven on earth, and we can see the majesty in creation, and so we really need to make that part of our life in some way that doesn't have to be saved for only the two weeks out of the year in some vacation spot.

So part of the "Life-lesson Love-lesson" for the twenty-first century is on the inside and part of it's on the outside. The inside is a daily routine of silence and prayer and meditation, which doesn't exclude any kind of spiritual reading. It can include it, but know that the main teacher about love in your life is going to be your prime lover, God, and that that essence itself will uncover what is not you. You can accelerate it by doing it more often. You can accelerate it by the act of humility, which says wholeheartedly in a decision, "Anything that I said about me, about others, about my family, about my job, about money, about life, about government, about sex, about fame, about power is not the whole thing, is not complete." Because if we fix on what we know, we've put on blinders. We've eliminated the scope of understanding. True understanding comes from inside, not from the outside.

This age of compassion—as I think somewhere in the future we're going to name this time in life—is probably going to spring out of people waking up to the suffering. I think a lot of the suffering that we have in life is unnecessary and comes from ignorance. To me, ignorance is not bliss, never has been—it's just stupid. Ignorance says either we don't want to know anything different or we know enough, and in either case we will remain either misinformed or uninformed about truth. We'll then make decisions out of that misinformation or no information, and then have inappropriate actions and behaviors in our lives. We'll continue being righteous, being self-ordained as, "I know what I'm doing; I'm in control; this is the way I want to do it; this is me—take it or leave it," and people around us will suffer. These expressions age you, strip away the spirit of joy and peace right out of you, and I think that there's a huge message that's coming out of the suffering that's happening in third world countries. There's a huge message in the people of Eastern Europe who are struggling because they finally have now broken away from control, but have no way of creating independence. We on the other side of the ocean have had independence and have abused it, and so what has happened is more control is being imposed upon us because of our abuse.

All of these levels of pain and suffering in humanity are, I believe, a huge spiritual wake-up call, and the call is the same message that was spoken to the prophets of the Old Testament, to Abraham, to Moses. It was the same message that was spoken two thousand years ago. It's the same message over and over, because, I think, the skull is still a little layer too thick, and this message is, "Seek first the kingdom of Heaven and everything else shall follow. The kingdom is within."

The wake-up call is to reclaim your identity. The wake-up call is to set free all of the falsified information you've stuck on yourself, like layers and layers of wrappings of Contac paper used to line kitchen cabinets, that are serving you to no avail. And we are bumping and bashing into each other at an opinion level but not at a truth level. Most of our arguments are about opinions, whereas truth needs no defense—it simply is.

There's a word from the Hebrew and the Greek, *hesychia*, which at first gets translated as the word *mercy*.[59] It is where we will oftentimes hear the prayer "Lord, have mercy," and centuries ago there were a group of what we would call now meditators, and they were called the *hesychists*. These people were people who spent time in silence, and the reason why they got the name *hesychists* is because in that experience of going within and being silent, they actually learned to feel the truth and presence of God. And the word we use now, *mercy*, is kind of like a watered-down translation of the word compassion. And when we say to ourselves, "Lord, have mercy," it is a prayer of the heart and a prayer of the soul that is not pleading, "Have pity on me." It is not pleading, "Have good favor on me." It is not pleading, "Please choose to save my wretched bones today." What it is saying is, "Show me your passion." The word *compassion* has a prefix *com*, which means "with," and the root word *passion* comes from the Latin *pax*, which is peace, and the real word *compassion* is kindred to our word *passion*"

We have not been taught to be passionate with our God. We have been taught to be light. We have been taught to be serviceable. We been have taught to be holy and reverent. But we have not had the freedom to feel passionate with our relationship to God, and I believe

59   George Maloney, S.J., *Prayer of the Heart* (Notre Dame, IN: Ave Maria Press, 1980), 22-24.

unless we free up and be passionate with God, we cannot become passionate with others. When I live my passionate life, which has more to do with my relationship with God than it does with being Italian, I feel the presence. When I feel the presence in me, I am able to feel the presence of God in you, and this is what enables us to love one another in peace. We must be passionate in our lives, to live life with an intensity, with a fire—a "fire in the soul," says Joan Borysenko, the author of the book *Fire in the Soul*.[60] We must live life with that kind of an intensity, which is not about pain but about joy. It's about celebration. It's about really feeling, "I am good; I am safe. I am important in this life because God designed me and placed a signature on my soul that promises no matter what happens in any given hour, in any given day, it is serving the whole and my job is not to be concerned about predicting a viable outcome, but my job is to be compassionate, to walk the earth as peacefully as I can, in all things great and small." I want to live with that kind of passion. I can't if I can't resource myself from the passionate one that is God within me.

Our faith must be alive and feeling and available and joyous and celebrating, and part of this age that I think we're moving into is to bring back the ability to feel, and sometimes the ability to feel first happens out of a pain, out of a crisis, out of a horror, out of a tragedy, because out of that you recognize you have no control and you are forced to go in deep, deeper than before, and find courage and find a way out. So the personal tragedies that you might have experienced over these couple of years were actually to get you to feel the presence of God in a more meaningful and deeper way and to set you free to live a passionate, alive, joyful life.

What we're going to see more and more in this decade is people talking about experiences and then at the end of the story, at the end of the retelling of this story—whether it's about love, whether it's

---

[60] Joan Borysenko, *Fire in the Soul* (New York: Warner, 1993).

about career changes, whether it's about being at the right place at the right time—is that people are going to say, "I know it was the hand of God that moved me in a way I couldn't have orchestrated myself," and it's going to liberate them out of their emptiness and out of the void, out of the hole in their soul.

The sign of the times is going to be a balance of suffering and compassion. Unless we reach out in all ways to go and help, to embrace and to serve one another, we are not going to know how good God is and how when you least expect it, whatever it is that you need, it will be given. There will be more prayer time. There will be less emphasis on structured religions and more emphasis on the freedom of spirituality. There will be more openness and acceptance to talk about God of the heart and how it feels when you pray, when you sing, when you dance, when you serve, as opposed to proving the existence of God.

We are, I believe, on the brink of a major change, and the reason is that we have more people with their "lights on" in their hearts than ever before. We've spent nearly thirty years in self-development, in the development of the true self. Finally now we are about ready to put the light on top of the table—and not under the bushel—so that everyone can see it. What is going to help us dissolve fear is to reach out and really be able to help each other. We will first go through the doorways of some pain, like a birth, and then there will be celebrating. The suffering does not have to be prolonged. The suffering is as long as you are holding God at abeyance.

In the earlier exercise, you might have remembered an experience that was trying to get you to go deeper in yourself, trying to challenge you to see that the truth about it is you don't know it all and the way that you see things is not the whole total picture. And for whatever reason, your anger, your depression, your pain, your sickness, your grief, your economic condition stopped you from taking the next step, and probably blaming God kept away the very power that you needed. The presence of God can't go away any more than you have power over your own breathing in terms of starting it or stopping it for extended periods of time. We can't do that. The power is ongoing. It's endless; it's ceaseless.

And the question that I think is going to be asked of everybody—regardless of where you've been in your life—in this next decade is this question: "Who would I be if I weren't so afraid?" Somehow, you're going to ask that question. You will ask it after an experience or before one, but the soul is going to demand this time that it be answered. I won't answer the question. The one within you has to answer it in a way that you will know you could not have orchestrated. I can help facilitate the soil so that you can hear it clearly. Think it now in your head: Who would you be if you weren't so afraid? Sometimes the next question right after that is: "Afraid of what? Afraid of whom?" Who would you be if you weren't so afraid? Right there it implies that you have an image of yourself without fear, because you're setting it up. "Who would I be if I weren't so afraid?" If you fill that in, you might recognize, "Well, I would do this and I would be this, and I would do this and I would do this, and I would feel this and I would do this." Well, I believe that who you would be if you'd let go of the illusion of fear, let go of the insane judgment that we put on ourselves, called guilt, is you would be just as God created you: significant, talented, vibrant, needed, needing to learn more about love, perfect with all your flaws—a real, vital source of change on the planet.

I want to include an excerpt from *A Course in Miracles* that talks about who would I be if I weren't so afraid and then I want to end with an exercise that will help you to answer the question alone and intimately, privately, with your own God and your own naked self. The quote is from chapter 31 in Volume I of *A Course in Miracles*, under the passage "Choose Once Again." It reads:

> The images you make cannot prevail against what God himself would have you be. Be never fearful of temptation

then, for see it as it is, another chance to choose again, and let Christ's strength prevail in every circumstance, in every place you raise an image of yourself before, for what appears to hide the face of God is powerless before his majesty and disappears before his holy sight. The saviours of the world who see like him are merely those who choose his strength instead of their own weakness seen apart from him. They will redeem the world, for they are joined in all the power of the will of God, and what they will is only what He wills. Learn, then, the happy habit of response to all temptations, to perceive yourself as weak and miserable: "I am as God created me. His son can suffer nothing and I am His son, I am His daughter."

Your Worksheet B

In this exercise, let your own naked self hear from God, from the voice, from the presence, who you really are.

- Close your eyes and allow yourself to be comfortable. Take your time in breathing in this exercise. Know that with every breath you take, you draw closer to God. Close your eyes and keep them closed. Every breath you take, you draw closer to a holy and reverent place where God awaits. Every breath you take, you undress yourself of all the illusions, all the preconceived notions of weakness, victimization, pain, hurt, blame, that you have placed upon yourself.
- At the count of three, you will imagine yourself in a holy place. You will decide where that is and you will be alone and naked—naked of all the opinions, ready to see yourself anew, and you will be before your God. One, two, three. Let an image of the presence of God come to you. For some it is a being of light; for some it is a soft and peaceful feeling. Let

it come on its own. Notice your first feeling. Is it relief? Is it sadness? Is it guilt? Is it anger? Is it depression? Is it blame? Is it loneliness? Is it pain? And know that all of these feelings must come to the surface of your consciousness so they may be removed. The illusions must fade so that in the silence you can hear and sense and feel only the voice and the presence that is God. Listen in silence as you ask of God: "Who would I be if I weren't so afraid?"

- Be still and listen, and know that who you would be is safe, always surrounded by the presence of God's love—guiding you, directing you, and protecting you in all things great and small. You'd be free just to be. You would be the resurrected you, the enlightened you, the God-like you, and in this you would be an example of Heaven on Earth. In this, let peace reign.

- When you're comfortable to do so, open your eyes and remain silent to give yourself time to reflect on these feelings and images. Repeat this exercise on your own several times. Keep notations, like a journal or a diary, so that you can come to really know that who you'd be if you weren't so afraid would be you—the safe you, the resurrected you, the wholesome, miraculous you, the peacemaker.

The more that you ask that question in that silent and holy place inside yourself—"Who would I be if I weren't so afraid?"—the more that you will peel off the layers that you erroneously and insanely put on yourself, the more you're going to realize you have been subjected to your own judgment and that who you are is good and holy and kind and loving and talented and free. Centuries from now, they'll write about us and they will say, "In that age of compassion, that was the generation that allowed for resurrection now."

Bibliography

Barnes, Michael L., and Robert J. Sternberg. *The Psychology of Love*. New Haven, CT: Yale University Press, 1988.

Borysenko, Joan. *Fire in the Soul*. New York: Warner, 1993.

Bradshaw, John. *Home Coming*. New York: Bantam, 1990.

—*Creating Love*. New York: Bantam, 1992.

Branden, Nathaniel. *The Psychology of Self-Esteem*. New York: Bantam, 1969.

Chopra, Deepak, M.D. *Quantum Healing*. New York: Harmony Books, 1989.

—*Ageless Body, Timeless Mind*. New York: Harmony Books, 1993.

Csikszentmihalyi, Mihaly. *The Evolving Self: A Psychology for the Third Millennium*. New York: Harper Collins, 1993.

Curtis, Donald. *How to Be Great*. North Hollywood, CA: Wilshire, 1978.

Des Roches, Brian. *Reclaiming Your Self*. New York: Dell, 1990.

Feshbach, Seymour, and Bernard Weiner. *Personality*. Lexington, MA: D. C. Heath, 1986.

Forward, Susan, Ph.D. *Men Who Hate Women and the Women Who Love Them*. New York: Bantam, 1986.

Foundation for Inner Peace. *A Course in Miracles*. Farmingdale, NY: Coleman, 1975.

Fowler, James W. *Stages of Faith*. New York: Harper and Row, 1976.

Freud, Sigmund. *The Future of an Illusion*. Translated from German and edited by James Strachey. New York: W. W. Norton, 1961.

Fromm, Erich. *The Art of Loving*. New York: Harper and Row, 1956.

Gawain, Shakti. *Creative Visualization*. New York: Bantam, 1978.

Gibran, Kahlil. *The Prophet*. New York: Alfred A. Knopf, 1923.

Grof, Stanislaw, M.D. *Holotropic Mind*. New York: Harper Collins, 1990.

Harper, Robert A. *Psychoanalysis and Psychotherapy*. Englewood Cliffs, NJ: Prentice-Hall, 1959.

Hay, Louise L. *You Can Heal Your Life*. Santa Monica, CA: Hay House, 1984.

Hendrix, Harville, Ph.D. *Getting the Love You Want*. New York: Harper and Row, 1988.

Holmes, Ernest. *The Science of Mind*. New York: Dodd, Mead, 1938.

James, William. *The Varieties of Religious Experience*. New York: Macmillan, 1961.

Jampolsky, Gerald G., M.D. *Loving is Letting Go of Fear*. Berkeley, CA: Celestial Arts, 1979.

—*Teach Only Love*. New York: Bantam, 1983.

Jeffers, Susan, Ph.D. *Feel the Fear and Do It Anyway*. New York: Ballantine, 1987.

Jung, Carl G. *Psychology and Religion*. London: Yale University Press, 1938.

Maloney, George, S.J. *Prayer of the Heart*. Notre Dame, IN: Ave Maria Press, 1980.

Maltz, Maxwell. *Creative Living for Today*. New York: Pocket Books, 1967.

May, Rollo, Ph.D. *Man's Search for Himself*. New York: Dell, 1953.

—*The Discovery of Being*. New York: W. W. Norton, 1983.

Peck, M. Scott, M.D. *The Road Less Traveled*. New York: Simon and Schuster, 1978.

Peele, Stanton. *Love and Addiction*. New York: Nal Penguin, 1976.

—*Diseasing of America*. Boston, MA: Houghton Mifflin, 1989.

Ray, Sondra. *Loving Relationships*. Berkeley, CA: Celestial Arts, 1980.

Riley, Glenda. *Divorce: An American Tradition*. New York: Oxford University Press, 1991.

Sagan, Carl. *Broca's Brain*. New York: Random House, 1974.

Sartre, Jean Paul. *Existentialism and Human Emotions*. New York: Wisdom Library, 1957.

Schiamberg, Lawrence B. *Human Development*. New York: Macmillan, 1985.

Siegel, Bernie S., M.D. *Love, Medicine and Miracles*. New York: Harper and Row, 1986.

—*Peace, Love and Healing*. New York: Harper and Row, 1989.

Silva, Jose. *The Silva Method Manual*. Laredo, TX: Institute of Psychorientology, 1969.

—*The Silva Mind Control Method*. New York: Simon and Schuster, 1977.

—, and Robert B. Stone. *The Man Who Tapped the Secrets of the Human Mind and the Method He Used*. Tiburon, CA: H. J. Kramer, 1989.

Stevens, Anthony, Ph.D. *Archetypes*. New York: William Morrow, 1982.

Stone, Robert, Ph.D. *The Secret Life of Your Cells*. West Chester, PA: Whitford Press, 1989.

—*You the Healer*. Tiburon, CA: H. J. Kramer, 1990.

Tillich, Paul. *Dynamics of Faith*. New York: Harper and Row, 1957.

Turner, Gordon. *An Outline of Spiritual Healing*. New York: Warner Paperback Library, 1972.

Williamson, Marianne. *A Return to Love*. New York: Harper Collins, 1992.

Young, Jeffery E., Ph.D. *Reinventing Your Life*. New York: Penguin, 1993.

CPSIA information can be obtained at www.ICGtesting.com
Printed in the USA
BVOW04s1835061214

378054BV00002B/4/P